From Stuck to Unstoppable

A Roadmap to Help Small Business Owners Move from Survival to Growth

Susan Riccobon

Small Business Rookie

Contents

Introduction

According to the World Bank's global business statistics, SMEs (small and medium-sized businesses) account for roughly 90% of all formal businesses worldwide. They also account for more than half of global employment and are a major driver of economic activity across countries at all income levels.

You're not "small" in importance just because your business is small in size. You're part of the 90% that keeps supply chains running, communities alive, and people employed.

I wrote *From Stuck to Unstoppable* for you, a business owner, to help you transition from feeling stuck in your business to becoming unstoppable through transformation.

With twenty-five years experience as a CPA, I have encountered many passionate business owners who, despite their busyness, often lacked a clear vision for achieving their goals and, as a result, didn't experience growth.

My book is your guide. A roadmap designed to give you the essential knowledge, mindset, and practical exercises needed to move your business from being stuck to becoming unstoppable.

It's not a how-to guide for business basics but more about developing the entrepreneurial mindset to help you face setbacks with resilience, think creatively in the face of challenges, and stay focused on your vision as you grow your business.

The road to success isn't always straight with any type of business. There will be challenges, uncertainties, and moments of doubt. But along the way, there will also be triumphs, growth, and opportunities you never imagined happening to you. The key to navigating this journey successfully lies in your mindset and approach.

You'll discover ways to boost your self-confidence and develop a working style that feels energising rather than draining. You'll learn how to grow your business without losing yourself — and how to trust your own voice in a noisy world.

The journey ahead is full of possibilities, and my book is here to ensure you have the strategies you need to make your business survive and thrive amidst the constantly changing dynamics of the modern business environment.

Take a breath.

Turn the page.

Your growth journey begins here.

Chapter 1
Signs of Being Stuck

tarting a business is like unlocking a world of excitement and growth, offering you control over your schedule and the opportunity to implement your own ideas and strategies into daily business practices. At the beginning of this endeavour, you start with enthusiasm; everything feels new and invigorating as you embark on this venture and develop your business concept.

"You have to fight through some bad days to earn
the best days of your life."– Herb Brooks

The first few months may go smoothly, and you might find the first year to be manageable, which is encouraging. However, many business owners eventually face a challenge: They hit a point where they feel stuck and struggle to maintain the same enthusiasm they had at the start of their business.

So, what are the signs of feeling stuck? One key indication is that your business isn't growing as you would like or as it did before. As a business owner, you might notice signs that you are stuck in your progress and might feel like you've given it your all, but your bank account is a bit lower than expected. Perhaps you had high expectations of being in a better position with your business, yet you feel trapped and can't see a way forward. You've invested all your energy into your business idea and built up momentum to a certain point, but now the drive has diminished, and the momentum has stalled. Perhaps you may find yourself wondering what it's all about and if you've made a mistake in starting your own business.

However, don't become anxious, as these are all natural stages in the life of a business owner. Being stuck isn't about giving up; it's about realising that you need to unlock new opportunities to survive and thrive. Being stuck can introduce self-doubt, which, in turn, can lead to negative thoughts and feelings, and later bad or rushed business decisions.

In time, you may start to question your decision to start a business, wonder if you were ready, or think that others might have been right when they said it wasn't for you. Consequently, negativity begins to invade your mind, and you find yourself questioning the path you chose. Unfortunately, these negative thoughts are counterproductive and hinder your progress.

The Cost of Inaction

Business owners who stay stuck often don't realise they are losing more than just time—they're losing momentum, opportunity, and confidence.

1. Lost Momentum

In business, momentum is everything; when you stop moving, you lose the energy you've built. A week of hesitating to make a business decision turns into a month of waiting, which becomes a year of stagnation.

2. Missed Opportunities

While you're stuck analysing what to do next with your business, someone else is launching; while you're doubting your offer, someone else is serving your ideal clients. Every moment spent waiting is a moment someone else is winning with your clientele.

3. Eroding Confidence

Inaction breeds doubt the longer you sit still, the more you question your ability, your idea, and your worth. Action, even imperfect action, builds belief, so don't talk yourself out of taking action.

Never Give Up

Many people in business feel helpless not because they're weak or incapable, but because they're under pressure in an environment that can feel unpredictable and relentless. Feelings of helplessness show up in the following ways:

- The weight of responsibility–for income generation, customer satisfaction, and team members

- Uncertainty and lack of control–with market shifts, competition, and technology changes

- Isolation–many business owners don't talk about their

struggles

- Financial pressure–spend funds for short-term gain not long-term growth

- Comparison to others–"I have no social media posts?"

To move forward from doubt and inaction, you must rise above feelings of helplessness. Everyone can make choices, and even when you feel stuck, it's essential to adjust your thought process to keep moving forward. Never give up.

I reached a point where I felt stuck and challenged, still a full-time employee for my regular job while attempting to start my part-time tax business. I initially thought I could handle both, but eventually I found myself stagnant, unable to dedicate enough time to my full-time job or my business clients.

There are only so many hours in a day. While running a part-time business is feasible for a while, there comes a point when you need to commit to your goals fully.

"Goals are like magnets. They'll attract the things that make them come true." – Tony Robbins

I chose to commit fully to my business, and that was the best decision I made, as it enabled me to write this book and become a business consultant. During my twenty-five years as a CPA, I have worked in both private and public companies, many of which are multi-million-dollar organisations. I chose to start my own business to be my own boss and implement my own ideas, rather than go through the layers of decision-makers as I had before. It wasn't until I started my own business that I truly understood what it was like to be a business owner. I have been stuck before, but what changed and gave me purpose to turn things around was the **change in me**.

Since my early twenties, I've read hundreds of books, articles, and blogs on self-improvement, a topic that interests me. These resources greatly helped me become more confident about what I wanted to do with my life. My first book was *Feel the Fear and Do It Anyway* by Susan Jeffers, which teaches you how to overcome your fears. The core idea of the book is **not** to eliminate fear, but to teach you to **move forward with** it rather than waiting for it to disappear.

At the time, I had spent four years studying accounting at Newcastle University in Australia, so reading Susan Jeffer's book was a breath of fresh air. Rather than learning how to apply my knowledge to help my employers, I was reading a self-help book to improve my self-confidence for my career.

From that day on, I have read many self-help books and listened to many podcasts, and I have also been inspired by Tony Robbins, an American coach and motivational speaker. I hope you find this book inspiring and that it helps you see new possibilities for yourself in your business journey.

It's essential to recognise that feeling stuck is a normal part of business. You may reach a point where growth in your business seems elusive, and that's when you need to step out of your comfort zone and seek ways to move forward again.

Many business owners mistakenly believe they will generate significant profits in their first year. They are enthusiastic, driven, and full of great ideas, but often, they find that these efforts provide little to no results initially, which can lead to disillusion-ment. However, I tell business owners during meetings that it's common not to see a profit until the third year, and this timeline is average.

Starting a business involves navigating a challenging path: if it were easy, everyone would be doing it, and there would be no employees, as everyone would be selling their knowledge, experience, or products.

For example, my husband and I operated an electric bicycle business before I started my tax business. We participated in a training session on importing products from China. At the time, we felt overwhelmed by the idea of obtaining a 40-foot container of product; realistically, we felt fortunate to have just a few bikes.

However, when we entered the electric bike business in 2010, I was so excited to tell a friend, "I've got an electric bike!" He replied, "Well, you'll be the only one on the bike path." I thought, *Wow, that's great!* However, we soon realised we couldn't compete with the big players in the electric bike market. Because of this, we became stuck because we couldn't sell at a price that would make a profit. Competing on price wasn't feasible, and we weren't established enough to compete on brand either.

By our third year of business, we were successfully importing 40-foot containers of our product as we gradually gained mo-mentum during the first two to two and a half years. This change was driven by a shift in our target market. Initially, we were focused on two-wheeled bikes, but as the market showed a need for tricycles, we pivoted our business, which turned out to be the best decision we made. Although we had experience as cyclists and knew our product well, the tricycle market was different to us. Once we shifted our focus, everything changed in our business.

With tricycles, we began meeting the needs of older individuals who faced balancing issues but wanted to continue riding to enjoy the benefits they provide. Many had enjoyed biking throughout their lives, and tricycles offered them a way to exercise and enjoy the fresh air as they did before. I felt elated when we sold a tricycle to a couple in their 90s. The husband appreciated it so much that he bought one for his wife, allowing them both to enjoy biking together.

By changing our thought process and listening to the market, we found a way forward. At the start of our business, each Saturday, we would wake up at 4 a.m. to prepare for our local market by loading our four electric bike models into our van. When we displayed our bikes at the market, people started asking if we had considered electric three-wheeled bikes. Until then, we hadn't thought of it, but I was so pleased that we listened to the public.

Eventually, during the COVID-19 pandemic, we decided to sell our business because our representative switched to a new manufacturer we weren't happy with, and all freight in and out of Australia was unpredictable. When the community was allowed to go out and exercise during the pandemic, we were able to meet that demand, making it a fulfilling experience. Interestingly, we sold all our tricycles and accessories during this time, leaving us with nothing to offer prospective buyers of our business. However, it wasn't solely about the financial aspect of a business sale; it was about the pride we felt in having established ourselves to the point where we could help others during a difficult time.

Ultimately, we looked forward to moving on to new endeavours, and this phase marked a significant chapter in our lives.

Our journey illustrates how adapting and responding to market needs can lead to success, even in challenging circumstances.

Pivot to Another Direction

I'm sharing my story with you because you might reach a point in your business where you also need to pivot. Think outside the box: What does the market need? Can you present the product in a way that differs from your competitors? You might even be in a market with no competitors, but if you are in a competitive space, it's crucial to listen to the market.

Identify the problems your product solves and understand the pain points of your customers. A pain point is a *specific problem, frustration, or challenge* that a customer experiences and wants resolved. A pain point is the reason someone is motivated to buy a product or service from you.

Take a step back and genuinely reflect on where you are and how you can pivot in a new direction for your business. One of the best ways to listen to the market is to join Facebook groups focused on your niche or offer similar products or services to yours. Ask questions about the difficulties people face or their satisfaction with the products currently available in the industry.

You can also search these groups for specific industry-related terms to find past discussions. For example, if you provide gym equipment, you could join a Facebook group that promotes exercise, wellness, and fitness and search for "gym equipment." You'll discover various and interesting conversations that can give insight into what people appreciate and identify areas for product improvement.

Being stuck is not necessarily a bad thing; it often signals that it's time to rethink your approach for success. Consider what changes you need to implement, who you should partner with, and whom you can consult for advice. This can be a turning point. Don't see being stuck as a reason to give up; it's an opportunity to innovate and move forward.

Throughout this book, I discuss my S.W.E.A.T. principles of strength, weakness, energy, action, and taking control of your future. These principles, which I will elaborate on in later chapters, will help you move forward in your business without giving up on your dreams and goals. Success is within your grasp.

A positive mindset is the key to success

Being stuck is a mindset that occurs when your brain seeks comfort and avoids exerting energy. As a business owner, it's crucial to take care of yourself and prioritise your health. You need to be prepared to face challenges and be in the best shape possible, so start your day by focusing on your priorities, whether that includes meditation or quiet reflection or other activities to find peace. It's essential to organise your day and commit to achieving at least one small goal to improve the business that you hadn't been doing in the past. This incremental progress is vital because, without it, you might fall into a negative mindset filled with "what-if" scenarios—what if this goes wrong? What if that venture doesn't work?

Instead, visualise the positive outcomes of your decisions. Believing that your actions will move your business forward is critical. While a "what-if" analysis can be valuable, ensure it remains constructive. For example, consider scenarios such as "What if I increase my price?" or "What if I approach this differently?"

and whether it will help or hurt your business. If you don't push forward, you may remain stagnant.

Make time for yourself and find a peaceful environment where ideas can flow, improving your business and yourself. Without this space, it's easy to feel trapped in negativity and see no path forward. Break free from that mindset by thinking creatively and implementing something new each day. For instance, before you read your emails and before anyone claims your attention:

- Write down three **priorities** for the day

- One for *money*, one for *growth*, one for *yourself*

It doesn't have to be a big priority; what matters is building momentum, day after day.

Consider your customers' perspectives when making decisions. If cash flow is a concern, consider ways to build up your funds to support your main business. Look for side opportunities that can complement your business while helping with cash flow. Some examples of opportunities are:

- Renting out assets you already own–great if your business has equipment, tools, or space (office, meeting rooms)

- Digital products and passive income–selling eBooks, how-to guides related to your industry; creating business templates such as contracts, forms, or planners; selling online courses or offering paid webinars or workshops

- Services you can add easily–VIP same day service, maintenance or monthly retainer services or consulting

- Products you can add easily–branded notebooks, pens, or mugs, starter kits (PDF), maintenance kits (cleaning, repair, essentials)

So, your main business gets to *grow* instead of just *keeping the lights on.*

Strengthen Customer Relationships

Having strong customer relationships is important because they're the foundation of business growth and long-term success. Here are the key reasons why:

Customer Loyalty and Retention

When customers feel valued and understood, they are more likely to stick with your brand. Building trust and a positive relationship makes them return, reducing the cost of constantly finding new customers through marketing and other channels.

Increased Sales and Referrals

Happy customers often buy more and return more frequently. They recommend your business to others through word of mouth, which is the most powerful and cost-effective form of marketing.

Better Understanding of Customer Needs

When you maintain a good relationship with your clientele, customers feel comfortable sharing feedback on what they like and don't like about your products and/or services. This helps you understand what they truly want, allowing you to improve your product or service and stay ahead of your competitors.

Competitive Advantage

Products and services can be copied, but customer relationships are unique. A strong bond with customers makes it harder for competitors to take them away with promises of better products and/or services.

Trust During Challenges

Every business faces issues—delays, mistakes, or problems that will affect customers. A solid customer relationship creates goodwill, so customers are more forgiving when challenges or mistakes happen, knowing you are genuine and have always helped them in the past.

Emotional Connection

People buy with emotion and justify with logic. When you connect with customers on a personal level, you're not just selling a product—you're becoming part of their life or business journey.

All the above shows that a strong customer relationship transforms simple transactions into powerful connections that could last for years and weather any challenge. Customers who feel cared for become loyal, even in difficult times, and often share their positive experiences with the world.

Starbucks and Its "Regulars"

Starbucks, for example, built its brand not just on coffee but on relationships. Baristas are trained to remember customers' names, favourite drinks, and even small details about their lives.

An important strategy for Starbucks is to engage with its customers and understand their needs. Conducting surveys, maybe twice a year, can provide valuable feedback on your products or services from those purchasing them. Making these surveys anonymous encourages honest responses, helping you identify what works and what doesn't. This insight is crucial, as your offerings may no longer meet current market needs. Uncertainty makes people more cautious and value-focused. In a tougher or uncertain economy, buyers' needs shift from **"Do I want this?"** to **"Is this safe, necessary, and worth the money?"**

For example, personally, a client from my accounting practice believed his business marketing was effective until he discovered a misalignment between the advertising message he developed and actual sales. He realised his Facebook ads were misleading and needed adjusting, which shows that sometimes small tweaks can have a significant impact on your business's success. By addressing issues based on feedback, you can boost sales, establish credibility, and attract positive reviews in the market.

Create Your Own Social Media Video

One way to reach your market is through social media. For example, I created a video for our CyclePower tricycles without a script. My husband and I decided to film at a park near our home to showcase a unique feature of our tricycle: its swivelling frame, which helps prevent a regular tricycle from becoming unbalanced and tipping over.

We found a path that wasn't straight but snaked around, making it perfect for the demonstration. I suggested we film my husband riding through this area, recording him explaining how our tricycle allows riders to lean into corners, like a bike. During the filming, I asked him to explain how the frame swivels, resulting in an additional ten minutes of recording in which he detailed the mechanics and how it worked.

The key takeaway from this example is that you don't need professionally produced videos for social media, whether you're showcasing yourself, a product, or a service. You don't have to spend a lot of money on professional services; in fact, rawer, more natural videos often engage viewers more. If you can articulate your message clearly, that is what truly matters. Sometimes, overly polished presentations can be distracting, causing your message to get lost in the glitz and glamour.

Our video, shot spontaneously without a script, received thousands of views and brought in business for us. I would often take calls from around Australia and receive international emails from prospective customers who said they had seen our video online and were interested in purchasing the tricycle. It proved to us that we could do it ourselves at little to no cost.

Another social media example was a customer's issue with assembling the tricycle after delivery. We would record a video with instructions and then upload it to Facebook to share with our current customers and anyone else. This spontaneous approach was beneficial for our customers, as it visually demonstrated what needed to be done to assemble the tricycle, giving them peace of mind and confidence in our ability to provide after-sales service.

I want to share this insight with you because you shouldn't feel pressured by anyone to spend a lot of money to convey your message. Perhaps this is where you feel stuck, wondering how to present your product or service without hiring professional services. I'm here to assure you that you can do it yourself, especially with a friend's help. Just get out there and do it! You'll enjoy the process and satisfaction of knowing you did it yourself.

Don't let a lack of cash flow hold you back. Confidence is key and sets you apart, while overthinking a solution can be a significant barrier to progress. We often second-guess ourselves, allowing negative thoughts to take over. This can lead to inaction, which we addressed earlier in the book. If you need to talk to a customer or contact a supplier for help, just do it—don't get stuck in hesitation or lack of creativity.

Embrace the freedom to make your own choices in your business, which is likely why you started your business in the first place. As you gain momentum, you'll see how you can grow your business, and that's an exciting journey. Being your own boss allows you to implement new ideas and pivot when necessary, and as a small business owner, you can make changes quickly without going through levels of decision-makers that larger firms require.

Small business owners often feel the pressure to do everything themselves; this is where having a business plan is crucial.

You need to recognise that you can't handle every task on your own, and it's essential to seek help. With this in mind, there are many affordable online services available, such as bookkeeping assistance, which can significantly benefit your business.

With bookkeeping as an example, learning it can be challenging, even with formal education, so it's essential to find support in that area. While using an Excel spreadsheet for managing your finances can work initially—especially if you're keeping track of cash flow—this spreadsheet can become insufficient once you start reporting for GST/VAT or other taxation requirements.

At this point, investing in dedicated accounting software is advisable. Utilising external services allows you to focus on what you do best: running and marketing your business and providing your products or services. Don't get caught up in tasks that detract from your core business. If managing Facebook ads or bookkeeping feels overwhelming, you can hire professionals to handle these tasks quickly and efficiently.

Getting stuck in trying to do everything is a common challenge for business owners, and help is needed. Facebook groups are an excellent resource for finding suggestions and connecting with other small business owners for advice. By observing their conversations, you can gain insights into the common issues they face. Starting a conversation in these groups can also lead to valuable support—after all, we're all in this together.

These groups are important because it's easy to feel isolated and overwhelmed as a small business owner. That's why it's necessary to be part of a community, whether it's your local business networking group or on social media. You won't have all the answers, but being connected to others can help you navigate challenges and discover solutions to ongoing issues. Let's see this advice play out in a fictional example about small-business owner David.

David's Story

David sat in the corner booth of the café. His laptop was open, but the screen taunted him with an empty Google Doc. He had been trying to write a blog for his new business for an hour, but all he could think about was how stuck he felt.

Two years ago, he left a stable job to build Eco-Furniture, a platform to help people find sustainable furniture. He believed in the mission—assisting homes to become greener—but lately, nothing seemed to move forward.

User growth had plateaued, cash reserves were draining, and the only emails that seemed to come through these days were bills. *Maybe I made a mistake,* David thought to himself, allowing his self-doubt to creep in.

The voice in his head was louder than ever: *I'm not cut out for this. Real business owners figure it out faster. Why is it taking me so long?*

Finally, he closed the laptop and stared out the café window. Across the street, a group of college students were cheerful and laughing as they carried chairs out of a second-hand shop. And then, something clicked.

They weren't buying new furniture at all—they were *upcycling.* Sustainability wasn't about new products for most people; it was about finding beauty in old ones, as this group was doing. David realised Eco-Furniture had been trying to sell what his customers didn't actually want.

He left the café and ran back to his apartment, where he started sketching a new concept: a peer-to-peer marketplace for upcycled furniture, complete with tutorials and local pickup options. Instead of competing with big-brand retailers, Eco-Furniture could empower creators and DIYers—the real champions of sustainability.

That night, David sent a bold email to his team: "We've been solving the wrong problem. Tomorrow, we pivot."

The following six months were chaos—late nights, new branding, rebuilding the platform from scratch—but this time, the numbers moved. Creators started signing up, influencers shared their upcycling hacks, and soon Eco-Furniture became a hub for sustainable design enthusiasts.

David felt that familiar spark of purpose return and felt excited for the future with this change.

He wasn't stuck anymore and had learned the most important lesson a business owner could: Being stuck doesn't mean failure. It's the doorway to reinvention—if you have the courage to walk through it.

Chapter 2

From Stuck to Unstoppable

History provides countless examples of high profile businesses that have shifted from being stuck to becoming unstoppable. Apple, now the world's most valuable company, was once on the brink of collapse. In the late 1990s, it was bleeding cash, its products lacked identity, and analysts were predicting its downfall. Netflix, celebrated today as a global leader in streaming entertainment, nearly disappeared when its DVD rental model was threatened by changing technology. Starbucks, loved worldwide as a symbol of coffee culture, lost its way when over-expansion diluted its brand.

"We must not allow the clock and the calendar to blind us to the fact that each moment of life is a miracle." – H.G. Wells

Each of these companies faced moments of being deeply stuck, yet each reinvented itself and went on to become unstoppable.

So, the real question is not whether you will get stuck as a business. The true question is: What will you do when it happens?

Reflection Question: Where in your business right now do you feel most stuck? (Revenue? Customers? Operations? Confidence?)

The first step to becoming unstoppable is to confront the reality of your current situation with your business. Unstoppable means continuing forward no matter what challenges appear. You keep moving with determination, resilience, and purpose—even when it's difficult, slow, or uncomfortable. Unstoppable is when your **why** is stronger than any obstacle. Too often, business owners downplay their circumstances, holding onto the hope that "things will turn around" and crossing their fingers without making the necessary changes. However, growth starts with honesty.

When Steve Jobs returned to Apple, his initial action was not to unveil a grand new vision. Instead, he faced the harsh truths head-on. He eliminated unprofitable projects, acknowledged the company's weaknesses, and publicly admitted that Apple had lost its direction. From this position of honesty, he was able to begin the process of rebuilding.

Reinvention Leads to Transformation

Yet honesty sometimes alone is not enough. Businesses cannot transform through critique alone; they need purpose. Purpose is the lifeblood of unstoppable businesses, large and small.

Call to Action: Write down your business purpose in one sentence. Not what you sell, but why you started your business. Purpose provides clarity, and writing things down isn't just about remembering—it actually changes how you think, process, and act. When worries or tasks are written down, they *feel* more manageable and help to reduce stress. You'll be more likely to act on things you've written down.

When owner Howard Schultz returned to Starbucks as CEO in January 2008 during its slump, he realised that the company had forgotten its soul. It was no longer about creating a "third place" between work and home where people could connect; it had become obsessed with rapid growth and profit. With this in mind, Schultz refocused Starbucks on its original purpose by restoring authenticity, craftsmanship, and the brand's emotional experience, and the revival began. Schultz's key moves to refocus Starbucks were:

- **Returned as CEO** to restore the company's original mission and values

- **Re-emphasised coffee quality** by retraining baristas and bringing back hands-on espresso craft

- **Improved the store experience** to feel warm, local, and welcoming again—not generic or "fast-food"

- **Slowed rapid expansion** by closing weak stores and focusing on thoughtful growth instead of just more locations

- **Rebuilt company culture** through employee support, training, and benefits to foster pride and connection

- **Reinforced Starbucks as a "third place"**—a comfortable space between home and work, built around community.

Once reality has been faced and purpose rediscovered in your business, like with Schultz and Starbucks, the work of reinvention begins. Reinvention is the bridge between stuck and unstoppable and does not mean abandoning your business model but rather transforming it for the future. Netflix could have clung to its DVD model, but it chose to embrace streaming when it was first emerging. Later, it could have stopped there, but instead, it reinvented itself again as a producer of original content, forever altering the entertainment landscape.

Reinvention requires courage. It is easier to cling to the familiar, even when it no longer works, than to step into the unknown. But the businesses that dare to reinvent themselves are the ones that survive disruption and thrive in new environments.

For many businesses, reinvention begins with innovation, which is not about technology alone but about rethinking how value of products and services is created and delivered. Apple, under Jobs, began designing not just functional computers but cutting-edge products that blended art and technology. The iPod was not merely a device for playing music; it was a reinvention of how people experienced music. The iPhone was not simply a phone but the reinvention of communication, productivity, and entertainment in one handheld device. Innovation transforms companies from stuck to unstoppable by giving them a fresh way to serve their customers and continue expanding on that freshness.

Reflection Question: What part of my business is outdated and needs reinvention?

Every system you improve within your business will bring you one step closer to unstoppable momentum. Customer focus is one step and is essential for any business. Many struggle in this area because they stop listening to their customers' desires, assuming that what worked in the past will continue to work in the future. Starbucks experienced difficulties when it became so focused on expansion that it lost sight of the core customer experience: enjoying coffee in a friendly setting. Its resurgence was achieved by listening to customers again, improving store quality, and reconnecting with what customers valued most.

In contrast, Amazon, the world's largest e-commerce and cloud computing company, became a dominant force not by chance, but through relentless customer obsession. Jeff Bezos, founder of Amazon, said, "One thing I love about customers is that they are divinely discontent" (*2017 Letter to Amazon Shareholders*). Bezos is pointing out that customers are **never fully satisfied**, even when things are already good. If you give them fast delivery, they will soon expect **faster**. If your website is easy to use, they will soon expect it to be **effortless**. It's **a built-in feature of human progress**, and Amazon has succeeded by anticipating and meeting those expectations for the ever-changing customer.

Call to Action: Pick 3 customers *today* from your customer list. Call them. Ask: "I appreciate your trust in me. What's one thing I could do better for you?"

The reason I emphasise calling your customers *today* is that to transition from feeling stuck to becoming unstoppable, you need to take action immediately—not later this week or next week. Life has a way of intervening, and what should be a call to action can quickly turn into a call to distraction.

Reinvention also demands operational clarity, meaning everyone in the organisation knows exactly what they are supposed to do, how to do it, and why it matters. This is where many businesses remain stuck not because the market is against them, but because they are weighed down by inefficiency. Teams duplicate effort, processes are outdated, and decision-making is slow. Toyota's philosophy of Kaizen, or continuous improvement, demonstrates how even small operational changes compound into unstoppable strength for a business. The key idea behind Kaizen is that everything can be improved, with a focus on eliminating waste and not requiring much investment (Wikipedia. org).

The Kaizen method requires everyone in an organisation to be proactively involved in improving the company. It's a bottom-up approach to problem-solving that empowers employees to take on new challenges for their company's growth. For smaller businesses, this might mean automating repetitive tasks, delegating more effectively, or cutting products or services that drain resources. Remember the 80/20 rule, where 80% of your revenue generation comes from 20% of your customers. Instead of treating everything equally, the 80/20 rule helps businesses allocate time and money efficiently. Look at your customer base to calculate the percentage relevant to your business. It may be 70/30 or 90/10 – but the principle remains the same. This concept comes from Vilfredo Pareto who observed that 80% of Italy's land was owned by 20% of the population. In business, it's often called the Pareto Principle.

Being proactive means taking action in anticipation of future problems, needs, or changes rather than simply reacting and creating anxiety by addressing problems after they occur. It involves taking the initiative to prevent issues before they arise, so you aren't making hurried decisions. You want to have a proactive, not a reactive, mindset to running and operating your business.

Call to Action: Use the P.D.C.A Cycle (Plan–Do–Check–Act) to implement a proactive solution for a task in your business that needs attention. The example below shows its use for a retail outlet business.

- **Plan:** Pick one problem area (e.g., long wait times for services/products)

- **Do:** Implement a small change (e.g., introduce a fast-track lane for customers)

- **Check:** Measure the result (e.g., average wait time dropped from 10 to 6 minutes)

- **Act:** If it worked, make it standard practice; if not, adjust and try again

However, no business can reinvent itself without culture, as culture is the invisible engine that powers momentum in a company. A toxic culture filled with fear, resistance, or apathy will sabotage even the best strategies. An unstoppable culture, on the other hand, thrives on creativity, trust, and resilience. Netflix, for example, has famously empowered its employees with freedom and responsibility through its "No Vacation Policy."

Netflix **doesn't track vacation days,** thereby allowing employees to take time off when they feel it's right and responsible. This provides:

Freedom: Decide when and how much vacation to take.

Responsibility: Make sure your work and team goals stay on track.

This trusts employees to act like adults, so as not to be micromanaged.

Another example that Netflix implements for its business is hiring "High maturity talent."

Netflix deliberately hires people who are self-directed and **don't rely on strict supervision**.

Freedom: Individuals decide how to execute their work.

Responsibility: They must deliver high performance and collaborate well.

This means fewer rules, but also **higher expectations.**

Unstoppable businesses invest not only in their products but also in their people, knowing that culture is the multiplier of every other effort they try to make.

Reflection Question: Is my team energised by my business mission—or drained by it?

While reinvention is critical, transformation does not happen overnight, as the journey from stuck to unstoppable is paved with small wins. Jim Collins, a business researcher, author, and leadership/management expert, in his book *Good to Great*, described the flywheel effect—the idea that massive momentum comes not from a single push but from consistent effort over time. At first, the wheel barely moves, but with push after push, it turns slightly more. Eventually, it spins so powerfully that it becomes unstoppable (2001). Businesses must embrace this principle. A small win—a new client, a product improvement, a process that saves time—can feel insignificant in isolation, but when compounded with other small wins, it generates unstoppable momentum.

The flywheel concept became so influential that Jim Collins later wrote a short companion book titled *Turning the Flywheel: A Monograph to Accompany Good to Great* (2019). This book further explains how to build a flywheel for your own business.

Call to Action: Identify one small win you can achieve in the next five days. Implement it. Celebrate it.

In my tax business, I created a Stripe account and started accepting online payments from my customers. This made it easier for them to pay and improved my cash flow with prompt payments. I celebrated by giving my husband high-fives. Reflect on how you felt about your small win, and create a list of additional small wins to build momentum for you and your employees. You're on your way to achieving your goals when viewing this list.

Remember your "why" – the purpose behind your desire to be the exceptional business owner you aspire to be. Share your wonderful qualities with others and be a source of support for someone who could benefit from what you and your business have to offer.

Your Mindset Matters

The more profound truth, however, in progressing your business is that becoming unstoppable is not just about introducing strategy or systems but about improving your mindset. A strategy without the right mindset is like a sailboat stranded in calm waters. No matter how exceptional the boat is, it remains motionless without the invigorating wind to propel it towards its destination. The small business owner who goes from stuck to unstoppable is one who chooses to think differently with a positive mindset, seeing setbacks not as permanent defeats but as temporary challenges and obstacles, not as blockages but as opportunities to innovate.

Those obstacles are not something that blocks their paths. They ARE their paths, and these business owners embrace change instead of fearing it. They treat failure not as a final outcome but as valuable feedback to improve. This mindset creates resilience, which, in turn, fuels perseverance.

Consider Apple again as an example. Its return to dominance was not simply a matter of product design but about a mindset shift that believed the company could still shape the future. Netflix's success was not just about technology but also about having the mindset to disrupt the market before others could. Starbucks' revival was not just about coffee, but about the mindset to reconnect with human experience. In each case, the unstoppable mindset was the foundation for reinvention.

What about smaller businesses? The principles remain the same for a big or small business. During the COVID pandemic, countless small business owners faced the terrifying reality of being stuck as the world stood still. Restaurants could no longer rely on in-person dining, gyms could not operate normally, and retailers could not depend on foot traffic. Yet many became unstoppable by pivoting, changing the direction of their revenue pursuit. Restaurants began offering delivery kits, creating entirely new revenue streams. Gyms launched online classes, reaching members far beyond their physical locations. Retailers embraced e-commerce and discovered national or even global markets. These were not billion-dollar companies with vast resources but everyday businesses whose owners chose resilience and reinvention over giving up on their businesses and dreams.

The 6 Steps to Becoming Unstoppable

1. Confront Reality – Face the truth by not pretending things are fine when they're not, no matter how painful.

2. Reignite Purpose – Your *why* is your wind behind the sail.

3. Focus on Customers – Solve problems and add more value, rather than just selling.

4. Simplify Operations – Clarity beats complexity. Document processes and procedures to look for new ways to simplify. Consider automating repetitive tasks.

5. Stack Small Wins – Progress leads to momentum.

6. Never Stop Reinventing – Adaptation to a changing environment is the key to survival.

Call to Action: Choose ONE step above and commit to it this week. Write in your journal the steps to take and the outcome you would like.

The path from stuck to unstoppable is not a linear one. It's messy, filled with setbacks, uncertainty, and hard choices, but it's also filled with breakthroughs, renewed energy, and moments of triumph. The business owner who endures this path discovers that unstoppable businesses are not those without problems but those who refuse to be defined by them. They do not wait for conditions to be perfect; they act in imperfect conditions with unwavering belief.

Ultimately, the journey from stuck to unstoppable is about creating a lasting legacy for your business to grow and thrive. Money matters, growth matters, but what truly drives business owners is the desire to build something that lasts. Legacies are not created by businesses that have never faced hardship. They are created by those who have faced hardship, reinvented themselves during it, and emerged stronger once the hardship had passed. Every challenge becomes part of the story; every setback becomes part of the testimony.

So, if you feel stuck today, know this: You are standing at the crossroads of transformation. One road leads to giving up, to staying stuck, to fading away. The other road leads to courage, reinvention, and unstoppable growth. The choice is yours. Lift your head, face the truth, reconnect with your purpose, reinvent boldly, celebrate your small wins, and adopt the unstoppable mindset. Your business is not finished—it is being refined. Your story is not over—it is just beginning.

Chapter 3
Core Principles

To be a successful small business owner or entrepreneur, you need a set of core principles that serve as a foundation for your daily decisions and long-term strategies. I developed S.W.E.A.T. as a framework for Strength, Weakness, Energy, Action, and Taking Control, for business owners to think smarter and work with purpose to achieve success.

> "A river cuts through rock, not because of its power, but because of its persistence." – James N. Watkins

My S.W.E.A.T. principles, which I will discuss in later chapters, complement this set of *core principles* that every business owner needs to incorporate into their business. These core principles are: Integrity, Customer Obsession, Adapting to Change, Creating Value, Discipline, People Over Profits, Continuous Learning, and Resilience.

Integrity

The first core principle is *integrity*. Integrity means always doing what you say you will do, building trust with customers and employees in the process. Trust is the strongest currency in your business. For example, if you promise a customer that you will send an email confirmation or return a call, you need to follow through with that promise. This communication is often the first interaction with your customer, so it is important to uphold those commitments as part of building that bridge of trust.

Be aware that an email is considered a legal document, so be cautious about what you commit to, as it can create expectations for delivery that you may not be able to meet. If you communicate clearly about what you will do and when you will do it, you position yourself as trustworthy.

Communication is crucial, and many businesses struggle with it. They use speed over accuracy, which leads to rushed instructions, unclear deadlines for product or service delivery, and incomplete details overall. The result is frustrated customers and staff, and a lack of confidence in the business owner. By focusing on timely communication, you can avoid misunderstandings and dissatisfaction. Many businesses fail due to a lack of communication, whether between managers and owners or among staff or even to their customers. On the other hand, strong communication can elevate your business and keep everyone on the same page.

Your reputation is built on how well you communicate. If you are known for being a good communicator, it will attract customers. People are busy, and the worst thing you can do is make a customer wait. When they ask for information, respond promptly; if potential customers are comparing quotes from 3 businesses, including yours, timely replies will play a significant role in their decision-making process.

Don't underestimate the importance of maintaining your integrity. Always do what you say you will do, for the customer and the employee.

Customer Obsession

The second core principle is *customer obsession*, meaning that every decision should add value to the customer's experience of your business, and you become focused on making that happen. A loyal and satisfied customer is the best form of marketing; they will spread the word about your business. Positive reviews and testimonials from these customers are invaluable and cost nothing—the only investment is your commitment to performing at your very best.

Consider how far a loyal and satisfied customer can take your business, helping you gain more customers in the process. Every decision you make should focus on adding value to the customer experience. Therefore, keep a record of the discussions you have with your customers to learn from their feedback and improve your offerings. For my tax business, I like to keep a journal where I jot down memorable details my customers share, such as anniversary dates, children's names, family members, and hobbies. Writing these details helps me remember them for future conversations, allowing me to ask about their family and show that I'm genuinely interested in their well-being. This practice not only aids my memory but also creates a stronger connection with my customers, as they are impressed that I took the time to write down these personal details to include in our conversations.

I suggest you buy yourself a journal and start writing down thoughts and insights from conversations. Our minds hold so many thoughts that it's impossible to remember everything, so writing them on paper is essential. I remember having chats with my friend at restaurants, and we would often grab a napkin to make notes on ideas we had for either personal or business matters. Unfortunately, those napkins sometimes ended up in the bin because we hadn't turned them over to see what was on the other side before throwing them away.

Instead of relying on scraps of paper, a dedicated journal allows me to keep everything organised and accessible. Also, when you write things down, it helps cement ideas in your mind.

Adapting to Change

The third core principle is being *adaptable to change*. Markets change rapidly, so it's crucial to remain flexible, test ideas, and adjust quickly without clinging to failing business strategies. I like to think of business pivots as much like the story of "The Thinker," a sculpture created by a famous French sculptor – Auguste Rodin (1840-1917).

Even in the late eighteenth century, the principles of business applied just as they do today.

Rodin was considered as one of the founders of modern sculpture. His art is known for its realistic detail and expressive emotion. So inspired by Michelangelo's art, Rodin produced his first life-sized male sculpture. However, he faced criticism from the public. They said his sculpture was so detailed that he must have created the cast directly from the model's body. Rodin chose to pivot and began creating his works either in small or oversized formats (The Thinker), thereby dispelling doubts about his artistic skills. In adapting to the market's perception, he recognised the importance of flexibility (adaptable to change) in response to criticism. Rodin's willingness to adapt to change allowed him to expand on other abilities.

When it comes to your own business plan, recognise when a product or service isn't working because it's important not to stay stuck or spin your wheels following the same path. If the market isn't accepting a particular product, consider removing it or adjusting your product.

Surveys, as mentioned before, can be an excellent feedback tool on whether a product/service should be kept or not. They provide an opportunity for customers to give true and meaningful insights, whether positive or negative.

In your surveys, avoid simple yes or no responses; instead, ask questions that require a more detailed response. Try not to be too specific in questions in order to leave room for issues you hadn't thought of. Understand customers' perspectives on what needs implementation to help your product move forward. Anonymous feedback often encourages customers to respond openly, while loyal customers, who want to see you succeed, will appreciate that you're seeking their input towards that success.

Frame your feedback requests around customer service; inquire about how you, as a business owner, can add value to their experience. You might be surprised by the responses you receive, and this approach has worked well for me in my previous business where I've found it to be quite effective.

However, whatever their response is, don't be discouraged by negative feedback; it is just as valuable as positive feedback. While it's nice to receive praise, criticism serves as a marker indicating what isn't working. View negativity as constructive criticism because if you can't pivot or change what's not working of your products or services, consider removing it from your offerings. Keep in mind the 80/20 rule as we mentioned earlier in the book: If 20% of your product or service is responsible for most of the negative feedback, consider eliminating that portion. However, if this issue affects a significant part of your business, it's important to examine it more closely to determine a better solution.

Creating Value

The fourth core principle is *creating value.* Instead of chasing money, focus on creating solutions that will make for a lasting experience for customers. The more value you provide, the more profit will naturally follow. It's essential to add value to your offerings, especially in a competitive industry. If your products or services are similar to those of your competitors, you risk competing solely on price. Large organisations that can leverage greater discounts or offer a wider range of services will make it even more challenging for you to compete on price in your niche market.

Instead, you should differentiate yourself based on the unique value that you, as a business owner, can provide to your customers that they can't get elsewhere.

One practical approach I have taken, is joining Facebook groups related to my core business (as I mentioned earlier in the book). Initially, I recommend joining as yourself and not as a business owner; this allows you to read the comments and discussions among group members without any pressure from being a business owner. For example, if you are in the business of making golf clubs, you might join a golf club community. You can search for terms related to your products or services within the group, which will help you navigate through previous conversations on the platform. By doing this, you may be surprised by the insights that emerge, such as discussions about what constitutes good customer service, which businesses are recommended in your type of service/product, and critiques of products or services currently available in the market.

Don't hesitate to join in and ask any questions that could shed light on your business opportunities. Your curiosity is the key to unlocking new insights and opportunities.

By reading these conversations, you can identify gaps and challenges that your target market is facing. This feedback is invaluable and can give you a clear idea of how you can address these issues within your own business. Once you have a strategy to solve these problems, you can reach out to potential customers and let them know how you can help with the issues they have.

It doesn't cost anything to participate in these online communities, and you'll be surprised at how many groups exist. Focus on identifying your market (what you are selling/providing) and engaging with those communities to understand their responses to existing suppliers and ongoing issues. Out of those interactions, you'll find ways to add value to the market.

Remember, it's not just about what you can do for your customers; it's about the problems you can solve for everyone. If you can address challenges more effectively than your competitors, and do so in a timely manner, your customer base will grow, and positive reviews will follow. Ultimately, the community will start to recognise and appreciate your efforts, leading you to be in business for a while.

Discipline

The fifth core principle is *discipline*. While dreams are inexpensive, the execution of those dreams is invaluable. Consistency in daily habits, tracking metrics, and following through on your business plans will provide better results than relying on sporadic bursts of inspiration.

Action is important to maintain motivation and positive thinking, but it must translate into daily habits to be successful. One of the main ingredients for a productive business is discipline in your daily routines to avoid a start-stop cycle. You need to maintain momentum, which can only be achieved by consistently following through with daily tasks and being disciplined.

A good daily habit to start with is to plan your day the night before. This consistent practice will help you set a direction for your day and carry that thought process throughout. It's not about having sudden bursts of inspiration; rather, the focus is on maintaining consistency and discipline, even when life throws obstacles your way during your day. If something disrupts your routine, ensure you get back on track without falling into a cycle of starting and stopping or losing momentum altogether.

Consistency in daily habits is a crucial principle; without it, you lack direction in your business. You must follow through on your plans. I like to use the *"right now"* mindset—don't overthink what action you need to take. If something requires immediate action, such as making a call, just do it right away. This mindset prevents your mind from negotiating whether or not to act on a task. By committing to immediate action, you avoid losing momentum and the drive to execute.

If I know I need to complete a task, I remind myself to do it *right now*. There's no negotiation, as I consistently apply this approach even to tasks I may lack motivation for but know are important. If you negotiate with yourself and procrastinate, you risk slipping back into a comfort zone where you avoid making decisions altogether. To be a successful business owner, for the first time or as an established business owner, you must make decisions and move forward; that's part of growth overall.

People Over Profits

The sixth core principle is prioritising *people over profits*. Treat employees fairly as a thriving team creates a thriving business. Balance humanity with financial sustainability. You may not have employees at the beginning stages of your small business, but as it grows, you will need to determine whether to employ full-time employees, part-time employees, or hire contractors.

This principle emphasises the importance of treating everyone you engage with in your business fairly, which starts with your own employees. Avoid micromanaging your staff; it simply doesn't work. I have worked for employers who micromanaged, and it often felt suffocating as their employee. You need to give your team space to grow and make decisions following your principles, while remaining approachable and maintaining an open-door policy for them.

Micromanagement can create an environment where employees feel hesitant to ask questions of their bosses, fearing they will be judged or reprimanded for not knowing something. Instead, establish a solid set of policies and principles for your team to follow. I find weekly meetings to be helpful and sufficient in our employees and myself understanding the business principles.

It's essential to manage based on outputs rather than inputs of work. What I mean is that if you assign someone a task or project, you should allow them the freedom to use their knowledge to complete it on time. Continuously checking on their progress adds unnecessary pressure on them, so focus on providing the inputs needed for them to successfully complete the project instead. Initially, some training may be necessary, which is perfectly acceptable, but after that, allow your team the freedom to grow and develop. As the business owner, your time and attention must focus on growing the business.

Another way to put people over profits is long-term thinking that avoids shortcuts that can damage your reputation. It focuses on building systems, relationships, and products that last: this should be part of your initial business plan, which is based on a long-term vision. Don't get caught up in the latest trends on the Internet if they don't align with your long-term strategy: avoid spending your time, energy, and effort on short-term solutions. It's crucial to assess whether these trends fit into your business plan.

Stay true to the high standards you set for your business, as these high standards foster excellence, enabling you to produce outstanding results. Also, the short-term decisions you make should contribute to your long-term strategy of success.

Additionally, embrace radical transparency which is going beyond normal honesty and involves sharing information freely, explaining decisions openly, admitting mistakes quickly, and encouraging others to speak truth without fear. Be open about your wins, losses, and the lessons you've learned from implementing your business ideas: hiding mistakes only exacerbates the problems. Transparency builds trust within your company, customers, and external stakeholders. Every successful business owner has made mistakes, so it's important to be resilient and recognise that these mistakes are stepping stones to discovering what works.

As you develop your business and introduce your own ideas, things may not always go as planned. If you dealt with a supplier, customer, or employee in a way that resulted in a negative outcome, don't be too hard on yourself. Acknowledge the mistake and take responsibility. Blaming others not only shifts focus away from the solution but also prevents you from learning from the experience and strengthening your business.

To find a solution to a problem, ask yourself how the mistake happened and what you can do to avoid it in the future; this may involve changing your approach or re-evaluating your decisions. Remember, the choice was yours, and it's essential to learn from what didn't work instead of giving up. The most successful businesses are often those that have made the most mistakes. For example, Thomas Edison said on his projects that didn't quite work the way he expected, "I have not failed; I've just found 10,000 ways that won't work" (https://www.azquotes.com/author/4358-Thomas_A_Edison).

Instead of seeing your mistakes as failures, see them as opportunities to grow.

Continuous Learning

A business grows only as fast as its owner. One of the best things you can do for your business is to keep learning about your business, which is the seventh core principle, *continuous learning*. Reading and research are vital because sometimes you need to dig deeper to find insight for the steps to make for your business.

To foster personal and professional growth, it's essential to seek mentors, ask questions, and never assume you know everything, as it's a mistake to think you have it all figured out.

For me, seeking mentorship from Tony Robbins has greatly helped my business journey. His insights have helped me navigate many challenging situations in my life, even if he wasn't aware of my specific circumstances. I remember going through a particularly tough time working while I was a full-time caregiver for my mother. The pressures became overwhelming, and I told my husband that I needed to attend one of Tony's live seminars—a 4-day event, "Unleash the Power Within," held in Sydney, Australia, that I thought could help me.

At this point, I realised that I needed to prioritise my own mental health in order to be there for my mother. Before, I always considered myself strong, but the weight of the caregiving situation was too tough to bear. I felt that attending Tony's seminar would offer me the mentorship and guidance I desperately needed.

One memorable experience at this event involved walking on hot coals. The hot-coal walk isn't about pain or danger. The fire walk teaches you that your mind—not your circumstances—limits you. Once you beat fire, everyday challenges seem small. Witnessing Oprah Winfrey do this on a similar event with Tony made me think about the challenge but experiencing it myself was empowering. In the atmosphere of the event, surrounded by thousands of attendees, I found a way to shift my mindset beyond fear to decide to do the walk.

Prior to attempting the walk, I confided in someone sitting next to me about my anxiety, sharing my fears that I could slip on the coals, since I had previously broken my ankle. In that moment, I realised I was merely letting fear create excuses to hold me back.

Thanks to Tony's guidance and motivational talk, I turned that fear into strength and empowerment.

The sensation I felt after completing the walk was exhilarating. By the end of the four days, I had transformed. It was a difficult decision to leave my mother during that time, but ultimately, I knew I had to do it for my own well-being. I needed to be strong to be there for my mother. I am grateful for Tony's program and the positive changes it brought to my life and my family.

It's a situation similar to what is advised during an airplane emergency. When the oxygen masks drop, you should put your mask on first before helping someone else. If you assist another person first and then have difficulty putting on your own mask, you may find that you cannot help either of you later. This example relates to my own experience caring for my mother.

I was seeking a mentor during a particularly difficult stage in my life. It wasn't so much from the perspective of a business owner, but more for my personal well-being.

Resilience

The final core principle is *resilience*, which is critical when facing the challenges every business owner encounters. All business owners experience setbacks, and the principles of identifying strengths and weaknesses, managing energy, taking action, and gaining control of your business are essential for fostering re-silience—both personally and within your business.

Life presents numerous challenges, as I have learned from my clients. I once spoke to one of my clients during a meeting, who said, "I've had so much happen in my life that I just don't think I can do this anymore. It's too challenging for me. I've faced so many disappointments and setbacks; I really don't feel capable of continuing." I responded by saying that we all experience disappointments and setbacks in our lives. It's a universal experience: no one is exempt from facing difficulties, whether within themselves or in their relationships with friends and family. Life is inherently challenging.

However, it's not about what happens to us; it's about how we respond to those challenges and how we grow as individuals. These setbacks shape who we become. The exciting aspect of being a business owner is the opportunity to face these challenges head-on and implement solutions that foster growth and resilience. This is likely why you became a business owner in the first place—to have the freedom to make your own decisions and choices.

Being a business owner empowers you to tackle challenges directly, leading to meaningful results and strength. Even as you achieve those results, you will experience a learning curve as your business gets better and faster at tasks the more they are repeated. When you get things right, it can be incredibly satisfying and rewarding, encouraging you to keep facing challenges. Ultimately, the most rewarding part is having the freedom to make decisions and take ownership of how you confront and manage those challenges, which is what makes the journey exciting.

In summarising, a successful business thrives by adhering to the following core principles:

Integrity

Build trust by acting honestly and following through with what you say you'll do.

Customer Obsession

Understand customer needs and consistently exceed their expectations.

Adapting to Change

Stay flexible and respond quickly to new trends, challenges, and opportunities.

Creating Value

Focus on solving real problems and delivering meaningful benefits, not just selling products.

Discipline

Success comes from systems, routines, and follow-through.

People Over Profits

Treat employees fairly as a thriving team creates a thriving business.

Continuous Learning

Stay curious, improve skills, and evolve the business through ongoing growth.

Resilience

Persist through setbacks, recover from failures, and keep moving forward despite challenges.

"Success is built from steady, focused action repeated every day."
– Susan Riccobon

Chapter 4
Develop Strength

I developed the S.W.E.A.T. principles as a roadmap to help small business owners grow in their business. The acronym S.W.E.A.T. stands for Strength, Weakness, Energy, Action, and Taking Control. Some of these principles are repeated from chapter 3, *The Core Principles*, to further emphasise their importance not only for business growth but also for personal growth. A business can only rise as high as its owner—success follows when the owner grows and implements the right strategies.

> "What lies behind us and what lies before us are tiny matters compared to what lies within us." – Ralph Waldo Emerson

The first letter in the acronym S.W.E.A.T. represents *strength*.

Feeling stuck in your business isn't a sign of failure; it's a signal. A message. A powerful internal push that something needs to shift. And more often than not, that shift starts with you—your mindset, your habits, and, most importantly, your personal **strengths**.

In this chapter, we'll explore how developing and leveraging your unique strengths is not just a tool for growth—it's the **way out** when you're stuck and can't move forward in success. We'll unpack how a strengths-based business can reignite clarity, confidence, and traction.

Developing discipline, which is a key strength, involves training your mind to consistently perform certain tasks. (as I mentioned in chapter 3). It's not only a matter of doing a task occasionally; you have to consciously commit to doing things in a certain way and by a certain time to get positive results. Another aspect of discipline is avoiding regret; you don't want to end up regretting your failure to exercise discipline in your life, leading to impulsive decisions.

You can begin developing discipline in small steps before tackling larger goals in your business. One suggestion is to start your morning with a routine that fosters discipline. When I was in high school, I found myself hanging around with the wrong group of friends, and deep down, I knew it wasn't right. At one point, a teacher entered the room and announced she would be stepping in for our regular teacher. She then expressed that she had read our individual academic reports and believed in our potential. I felt she was talking to me, though she was encouraging all of us to start fresh and embrace the opportunity to change.

I took that advice to heart and made a conscious choice to shift my behaviour and focus away from the wrong group of friends. I applied discipline to my studies and homework and became so committed that I would stay up late at night working on assignments, even when my mother would tell me to turn off the light and get some sleep. During that time, I felt that I couldn't rest knowing I hadn't reached my full potential, so I kept studying, pushing myself to do more.

In the end, I passed my exams and went on to University, obtaining a Commerce Degree with a major in Accounting. If I hadn't developed the discipline to persevere and make that choice to change in high school, my life would be very different today. I could still be following the wrong crowd.

Success isn't just about what you own; it's about *who you become as a person*. I am incredibly grateful to my teacher for changing my life and helping me realise that the power to change ultimately came from within myself.

Discipline is both a choice and a challenge; if it were easy, everyone would be doing it. However, if you want to achieve your goals and move from feeling stuck to experiencing greater success in your business and in life, you need to strengthen your discipline, avoiding procrastination and second-guessing. Once you commit to a specific path, discipline will help guide you along the way. Think of it like a river—you need to paddle to get to your destination. It requires effort and determination, but it's also a key aspect of personal growth because developing discipline is essential for reaching where you want to be next.

Confront Challenges

Another important strength character in personal development is resilience. Resilience is the ability to persevere when faced with challenges and obstacles you might never have anticipated. When these hurdles appear, you must be prepared to confront the challenges they present. For some people, resilience becomes an escape route; they find it too difficult and lack the strength to pivot for change—whether that means adjusting their business model or continuing to push through obstacles in life in general.

To clarify, I'd like to share a story told by Dean Graziano at the Tony Robbins seminar "Unleash the Power Within" about two businesses in Idaho, both in the food industry, that were operating during the COVID-19 pandemic. One owner threw up his hands in frustration, claiming it was too difficult to continue since he had no customers coming through the door. In contrast, another business, owned by two brothers, viewed the situation as a challenge and sought to innovate their business model in order to maintain customer engagement.

While the first business owner complained and ultimately closed his doors, the brothers decided to think creatively. They realised they couldn't focus on competition; they needed to ask themselves how they could get through this tough time. To meet this challenge, the brothers adapted their business by adding a drive-thru service, allowing them to serve meals directly to customers in their cars with social distancing applied. This innovative change led to their success, as cars would line up to be served, and it was so successful that they introduced it across 60 locations.

This is a great example of strength to face an unforeseen obstacle and using it as an opportunity to innovate. The brothers not only saved their business but also influenced other businesses to adopt similar practices, proving that resilience is about not giving up and finding new ways to overcome challenges.

I watched a great movie called *Hustle* (2022) during my flight to the U.S., about Stanley Sugarman (Adam Sandler), a hard-working but exhausted NBA scout for the Philadelphia 76ers, a U.S.

basketball team. He travels constantly, lives out of hotels, and is stuck in a career that's going nowhere. While travelling in Spain, Stanley meets Bo, a construction worker who plays basketball in his spare time and has great potential. When he brought Bo back with him to the U.S. to train, Stanley didn't receive support from his team and had to pay Bo's travel out of his own money and train him personally.

However, Bo had emotional baggage, anger issues, a fear of failure, and pain from the past. Stanley helped him face his fears through discipline, mindset coaching, gruelling training, and emotional support. Stanley showed strength in his ability to believe in others, even when they don't believe in themselves. Bo had to let go of his past and find the strength to control his emotions, not let them control him, if he was to move from a construction worker to a trained athlete. They both became a successful player and coach even after setbacks.

This movie is great for business owners as it demonstrates leadership and personal development. Both Stanley and Bo had to use their strengths to fulfil their dreams. Stanley's strength is belief in others, and Bo's strength is the belief in himself.

Focus

Another strength is focus. To have clarity about your direction, you need the strength of focus. Avoid distractions, such as shiny objects or groups that might lead you down a different path, as they are the opposite of focus. Concentrate on what you want to achieve in your business and be clear about how you plan to achieve it. A strong, solid focus is crucial, and nothing should interfere with that focus.

From a personal example, I ride a motorcycle, and focus is one of the primary strengths needed when riding a motorbike. You must remain clear in your focus because as soon as you turn your head and look away from where you're heading, you start to move towards whatever you are looking at. This can be dangerous, especially if you're looking at an object on the other side of the road. Therefore, as in business, you need a clear focus on your goals and intentions, making sure that every decision you make benefits your business and doesn't harm it.

Another important strength to develop is consistency. As I mentioned earlier in core principles, this comes through discipline. Consistency must be maintained every single day; you can't just show up one day and not the next. You need to be consistent in your attitude towards your business, as well as in your ideas and the discipline you implement in completing your tasks.

If you're not consistent, you may begin to negotiate with yourself about whether to take certain actions on any given day, which could be disastrous. However, when you are consistent, there's no negotiation or options. You know exactly what needs to be done, and you simply get on with doing it. Don't let your inner voice distract you from your goals.

Form Your Natural Habits

For example, I might say to myself, "Today, I think I'll just sleep in, or maybe I'll go to the gym. I might not commit to three times a week; I could just go two or three times a month." However, it's crucial to train your mind so that consistency becomes a natural habit, such as working out consistently would make me healthy and fit. Consistency is all about developing habits and ensuring they show up every day.

Another important habit I want to mention is communication. Many businesses overlook the significance of effective communication, but it is important for both new and existing customers, as it shows that you care about them and that you're there to address their needs (as I shared earlier in the book). Acknowledging communication, whether it's an email or a phone call, is one of the most important things you can do. If someone reaches out to your business, you should respond in a timely manner—ideally within 24 hours. If you can't provide an answer right away, it's perfectly acceptable to acknowledge their message and inform them of the date you'll get back to them with an answer.

Unfortunately, many businesses lose customers and fail due to inadequate communication. People want to feel valued and don't want to be treated like just another number. There are other businesses out there that will make their customers feel appreciated for reaching out, so don't let yours be overlooked.

Communication is key in every aspect of life, not just in business. You need to express how you feel, share your intentions, and explain what's going wrong in life and business—along with what's going well. Additionally, it's vital to develop your listening skills with customers and employees. You can learn so much by genuinely listening to what others say, which often leads to new ideas and insights.

When an idea works, it can be an incredibly gratifying experience. However, it's important to be flexible and question every decision you make on whether it will or won't work. Don't just adopt practices because they're popular; instead, assess whether they align with your business goals and how they'll enhance your sales or marketing strategies.

Small business success doesn't come from perfection—it comes from the incredible strengths you bring to the table every single day. Your discipline shows your commitment when others would quit, your resilience turns challenges into growth, and your focus keeps your eyes on the vision ahead. With consistency, you turn small steps into big victories, and through powerful communication, you build trust, community, and opportunity.

When you combine these strengths, you become unstoppable—a business owner or entrepreneur capable of not just surviving but thriving in business. Keep believing, keep pushing, and keep building—because you have everything it takes to thrive. Your success is not a matter of if, but when.

Chapter 5

Strengthen Weakness

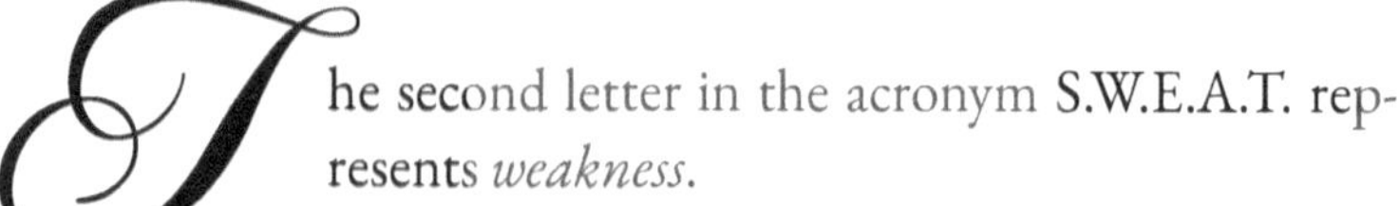

he second letter in the acronym S.W.E.A.T. represents *weakness*.

Weakness in a business indicates avoidance, fear, and lack of leadership clarity. Each of these factors, when combined, drains momentum and ultimately prevents growth.

"Our greatest glory is not in never falling, but in rising every time we fall." – Confucius

Let's dive into an important topic: removing weaknesses from our businesses! In our last chapter, we explored how to develop strengths, and now we will tackle the second part of our principles—addressing and eliminating weaknesses.

First things first, acknowledging that weaknesses exist in your life is a crucial step in the journey. Whether it's in your business or within yourself as a leader, this recognition can be empowering. Have you ever felt that initial spark of enthusiasm when starting something new, only to find yourself bogged down by negativity towards your abilities as time goes on? It's completely normal! Let's face it—many of us experience self-doubt, especially when we begin to compare ourselves with others in the industry.

When self-doubt creeps in, it can lead to questioning our motives and decisions, especially in business. You might find yourself asking, "What am I doing wrong?" or "Did I make a poor choice in starting this business?" It's okay to feel this way. The key is to recognise these feelings of weakness and know that they do not define your capability or your future.

Instead of letting self-doubt hold you back, let's turn that energy into a positive challenge! If something isn't working as you envisioned, don't hesitate to seek out help. The Internet is an incredible resource filled with books, articles, blogs, and podcasts that can guide you towards solutions. In my tax business, my weakness was poor communication with my clients. I would see them once per year, which created a lag in our communication and showed a lack of interest in them as important clients. I'm sure they would have just felt like another "tax return". After acknowledging this fact, I researched the Internet for effective communication techniques, which led me to introduce some changes into my business and communication.

I would send an email to each client about two months before the end of the tax year, informing them of any changes in tax law and offering tax-saving recommendations. I would ensure my messages were personal by including their name instead of "dear client."

Instead of merely doing the same task over and over again, ask yourself, "How can I do this better?" By focusing on what you can offer that adds value to the market, you'll set yourself apart and stay true to your unique vision while rising above the competition.

Now, consider this: Every time you encounter a setback or challenge, think of it as an opportunity for growth instead of a focus on your weakness. You have resources at your disposal, and by making small adjustments or tweaks to your current approach, you can attract new customers while also serving your existing ones better. It's all about solving the pain points in their lives!

Initially, when I started writing with a focus on employees, I struggled with chapter titles and the main points I wanted to convey. I had previously held a senior accounting position in both the private and public sectors, so I thought the ideas would flow easily for the book. However, they didn't; it wasn't until I shifted my focus to helping small business owners overcome their challenges that the ideas began to flow effortlessly. My chapter titles came together, and the topics I wanted to discuss became clear.

This experience made me realise that I had been focusing on the wrong area for my book and for business, as I needed to concentrate on the significant pain points and challenges small business owners face. Unlike employees, business owners often deal with more pressing issues and require more guidance. Employees have options and resources at their disposal, whereas small business owners can feel stuck and have to find help themselves.

By implementing the processes and strategies I developed, I turned things around for my small business, and you can do the same as I am sharing in this book. Consider who your products and services are for and try to move away from self-doubt as you have the capacity and capability to achieve your goals.

Facebook Groups

Take the time to write down your ideas and approaches instead of keeping them in your head. Write about your customers and their pain points and how your products and/or services help solve them. Overcome your tendency to procrastinate and take the time to list what you are struggling with.

One helpful strategy to overcome your weaknesses in business is to join Facebook groups within your industry. Share your problems and ask for advice; you'll be surprised by the responses. They will provide guidance and possibly mentoring to help you. This feedback can be invaluable. Think about how you can implement any suggestions within your own business. Don't be shy and ask for clarification if you don't understand what's being said.

Using Facebook for research can be powerful. Once you join a group, even if it's closed, it doesn't mean you have to start from scratch. You can search for specific topics and review past discussions. For instance, if you're looking into delivery time frames or how to get products to customers faster, just searching those terms will bring up relevant conversations and thoughts from this group's conversation thread. This allows you to gain valuable insights and better serve your customers or clients with what worked instead of what didn't. The insight not only addresses their pain points but also what they appreciate about those products and any feedback they may have since using them.

You don't even have to reveal your identity at this stage, remaining completely anonymous. However, you do need to have your name associated with your Facebook account, though you don't have to disclose that you are running a business. Spending time researching and reading, especially with online groups like on Facebook, is crucial, as it helps you acquire skills and knowledge that can further enhance your understanding of customers' likes and dislikes.

Remove Distractions

To achieve success in your business, you need to remove distractions, which can be weaknesses, and stay focused on your goals.

It's important to remember that, much like riding a motorbike (my earlier example), where you look is where you will go. If you turn your head while riding, your bike will follow that direction. Similarly, your business will move towards wherever you are focusing your attention. To avoid being distracted, which can be a significant timewaster, it's essential to establish clear boundaries and communicate your needs to those around you.

Say you're juggling a young family or caring for an elderly parent, it's understandable to feel pulled in different directions. In such cases, try to block out specific times in your day dedicated to your business, so those around you know when you are busy.

Remember, it's crucial to take responsibility for your own focus without blaming others for distractions. Instead of feeling frustrated when you aren't accomplishing things as you should, ask yourself how you can improve your situation. If you find that there are many distractions in your life, it might be time to rearrange how you allocate your time.

Some examples of common distractions that derail business owners are:

<u>Digital and technology distractions</u>

These steal time in tiny pieces but add up fast:

- constant email-checking

- phone notifications pinging every few minutes

- social media "quick checks"

- over-managing tools, dashboards, or logos

<u>People distractions</u>

Even well-meaning people can pull you off course:

- clients who text or call at all hours

- friends/family interrupting work time

- networking that doesn't lead anywhere

- meetings that should have been emails

<u>Internal distractions</u> (the most underestimated!)

These come from inside your mind:

- overthinking instead of acting

- perfectionism

- worrying about what might go wrong

- jumping to new ideas mid-task

- shiny object syndrome (Internet promotions)

- negative self-talk drains focus

- daydreaming or drifting to unrelated tasks

Here is a **simple, realistic, business-friendly, distraction-proof work routine** you can start using tomorrow. It limits interruptions, reduces mental clutter, and keeps you focused on what actually grows the business. After a couple of weeks, this will become your daily routine and will feel natural. You need to apply your strength of discipline to make this routine effective.

Start your day with a 10-minute "Control Your Day" Routine

Do this before checking email or messages.

- Review your top 3 priorities.

- Identify ONE task you *must* finish today.

- Clear your workspace (2 minutes).

- Turn off notifications or put your phone in another room.

This prevents you from getting sucked into other people's agendas.

Use the 90/20 Deep Focus Cycle

This is the core of your distraction-proof routine.

For 90 minutes:

- Work on *only one* high-impact task

- No phone, no email, no social media

- Close all tabs except the ones you need

- Use noise-cancelling headphones or focus music

Then take a 20-minute break to reset your brain:

- Quick walk

- Stretch

- Water + breathe

- Step away from screens

You can do 1-3 of these cycles per day.

3. Contained Communication Windows (Very Important)

Business owners often get derailed by messages.

Set fixed times for communication:

- **11:30 a.m - Check email/messages once**

- **4:00 p.m - Final check + replies**

Outside of these times, your emails stay closed. This alone can free 2-3 hours a day.

4. Daily "Friction Removal" (10 minutes)

At the end of your focused work block, or during mid-afternoon:

- Prep everything for tomorrow

- Close tabs

- Tidy workspace

- Write down tomorrow's first task

- Reset reminders & alerts

This sets you up to start fresh and focused the next morning.

5. Scheduled People Time (Avoid Random Interruptions)

Choose 2 windows to be "available":

- One in the late morning

- One in the late afternoon

Tell employees, partners, and clients: "Unless it's urgent, let's save questions for our scheduled check-in today. I'll be able to have a greater discussion with you."

This stops constant drop-ins or unnecessary calls.

6. The "No New Ideas Until Friday" Rule

As ideas pop into your head:

- Write them in a notes app or journal

- Review them **only on Friday**

This prevents shiny-object distractions from the Internet during the week.

7. Protect Your Energy

You can't focus if you feel drained.

Add daily energy habits:

- Morning walk

- 10-minute meditation

- Stretching

- A healthy lunch

- Hydration

Higher energy = fewer mental distractions.

8. Weekly Reset Routine (30 minutes every Monday or Sunday night)

- Review your goals

- Choose your top weekly priorities

- Block out deep work times on your calendar

- Schedule meetings

This keeps your week structured, not scattered

If you are working full-time while trying to build a part-time business, as I once did, distractions may come from both areas. You have to evaluate whether your full-time job is interfering with your small business goals or vice versa. If the distractions are coming from your full-time job, consider making a change, like working one day less each week if your job has this flexibility. This could free up an entire day for you to devote to your business, and you may be surprised at how much you can accomplish in that time.

Stay disciplined in your focus. If you have a blog to write as part of your small business but find yourself tempted to watch a great TV program, remind yourself to stay on track. If you allow yourself to deviate once, it becomes easier to do so again, and before you know it, you'll have missed another opportunity to make progress. Whatever you decide to do, ensure that you follow through without making excuses. Discipline and focus are key to success.

Planning is a crucial aspect of running your business, and you may find yourself stuck because you lack a clear plan. It's essential to have direction, so I cannot stress enough the importance of writing things down as you create your plan. Get your thoughts out of your head and onto paper. Invest in a nice journal—something that resonates with you and feels meaningful; this book will become an important part of your life. Keep your journal with you every day.

Whether you place your journal in your handbag or briefcase, make sure it's always close at hand. You never know when you'll be out with friends and a great idea strikes, as I shared about my lunches with my friend. Write down your ideas, aspirations, and vision for your business in this journal. Even if you feel stuck right now, moving forward starts with having a clear vision or plan of what that looks like.

It's not enough to move forward aimlessly; you need a plan. What is your end goal? What do you want to achieve? Visualisation is a vital part of this process. If you can't visualise your destination, how will you know how to get there? Instead of thinking, *My business is stuck*, think, *I see the future where my business runs smoothly, and here's the path.*

When the going gets tough, you need more than just financial gain. In your journal, write down what success means to you. Is it franchising? Becoming a #1 bestseller? Building the most successful business in your industry? Is it about travelling more or buying more property? You need to have that prize at the end in mind, and remember, it's not just a dream—it's a vision. There's a significant difference: a dream is simply something nice to have; a vision is as if you already have what you want, and you *feel the emotion it brings.*

This vision will help you move forward when you face challenges in your business. So, in your journal, clearly define what success looks like for you. Don't just keep it in your head; writing it down helps it gain momentum, which will drive you forward. If you find yourself stuck, looking at what you've written can help. Keep your end goals in sight as well, as you can achieve this through the choices you make. If you make mistakes along the way, that's okay. Even Edison made a thousand mistakes before figuring out how to turn a light on.

When challenges arise, having a clear image from your journaled ideas of what success looks like to you will provide the resilience needed to keep going. Have you considered what success means in this journey? When you reach your goal, what will that look like? How will you know you've been successful? Success is about who you become throughout the process—not just what you acquire. Consider what that transformation looks like for you through your words and vision. Remember, it's more than just making more money; success is much deeper than that.

Lost Momentum

Do not be discouraged by setbacks; learning from your mistakes is what makes you successful and overcome your weaknesses. No one in business has succeeded without making mistakes. It's about who you become through those experiences, and that growth follows you into every aspect of life.

In relation to employees, if you're feeling challenged by your staff situation, consider the reasons your employees might be leaving your business. Don't blame the economy or your competition but look more internally into how the business is going. For instance, if one of your employees wants to pursue a photography career while your business handles construction, perhaps you can create a role that allows the employee to express that passion within your business. Photography is vital for marketing and can evolve into video work as well if that is a business need.

You need to understand your employees' motivations for wanting to leave, as it's often not just about money. Many employees leave their jobs due to dissatisfaction with management; therefore, it's crucial to believe in effective management to be successful and keep employees happy.

Whether you work with employees or contractors, maintaining clear communication is essential for everyone. If you've chosen to operate with contractors instead of hiring full-time staff, it's vital to keep lines of communication open due to the shortness of time together. Establish transparent communication channels and promptly address any issues. Procrastinating can lead to significant problems, including the loss of key team members.

If you have doubts about your management style, implement an anonymous feedback system immediately for your employees. This approach allows every team member, including senior management, to voice their thoughts honestly. Anonymity is vital—it will encourage genuine feedback, both positive and negative, which is essential for pinpointing areas that need improvement.

This is necessary as you may think your business is running smoothly and that everyone is content, but there could be serious issues lurking beneath the surface. To drive continuous growth and ensure the success of your business, prioritise your team's feedback and take decisive action when needed. Your organisation's future depends on it.

Confront Your Fears

If you think you can run a successful business while ignoring the feelings of fear to take on a challenge or task, think again. Fear is an emotion that can stop you in your tracks. It's essential to understand that feeling fear is normal in business, acting as a trigger in prompting you to pay attention.

However, fear needs to be conquered because if you don't face your fears, you won't move forward or grow. Remember, you had fears when you started your business, so don't let them hinder your progress now months or years down the path. Many people, when faced with fear, retreat to their comfort zone to stay calm. While the comfort zone can feel safe, nothing ever grows there.

If you want to move forward and achieve growth, you need to confront your fears directly. Once you've conquered them, you'll look back and realise that facing those fears was simply a journey you had to undertake. Embrace the idea of feeling fear and doing what needs to be done anyway to conquer them. Recognise that it's fear but proceed with what needs to happen. If your fear is about making mistakes, remember that you will likely make mistakes along the way. However, there are valuable lessons to be learned from them, as every successful business owner has faced setbacks and made mistakes.

Fear can also serve as a wake-up call. If you don't address it and move forward, it becomes a weakness—running away from fear. For instance, if you fear starting a podcast for your business, do your research to know how to start and operate a podcast. You don't need to reinvent the wheel; find out what works for others and adapt it for yourself.

You'll discover that once you start, you'll gain momentum over your fear. The hardest part is often just starting; it's less about the task itself and more about the fear of beginning. If you can block out that fear and take the first step, you will be on your way to moving forward.

Everyone experiences fear, but what matters is how we respond to it. That little voice of self-doubt can lead to statements like, "What if this isn't successful?" or "What if I fail?" But consider the alternative: "What if it turns out to be great? What if it becomes the best decision I ever made?"

Create a vision board with photos, images from magazines or the Internet and quotes. A vision board is a visual representation of your dreams that you can look at to feel inspired and focused on your future. Look at your vision board often and focus on your goals.

If you need to confront fear, do so, but don't get overwhelmed by the big picture. Break it down into smaller steps if necessary. Recognise that overcoming this fear is a challenge, but don't shy away from it; move towards it. Implementing small steps makes the process less daunting and more manageable.

Start now, because the sooner you begin, the closer you'll get to fulfilling your dreams.

80/20 Rule

Don't fall into the trap of trying to please everyone and doing everything for them. This is a common weakness, people-pleasing; while you might be pleasing others, the only person you truly need to please is yourself. The 80/20 rule applies to many situations, including your customers or clients. Typically, 80% of your income comes from just 20% of your customers; therefore, you shouldn't waste your time and energy on the remaining 80% who aren't contributing to your business's growth. Instead, focus on that crucial 20%, as these clients are the ones who will promote your business, leave positive reviews, and generate momentum for your success.

Learn to say "no" to most of the 80% that drain your time and energy, yet it's important to do this graciously and without guilt. If you feel guilty about saying no, you may end up saying yes to everyone, even if you don't genuinely want to. This cycle is not a good business practice, so a better approach is to say you can't now but will see if an opportunity arises later. Don't say yes and put pressure on yourself to deliver.

Stay strong in your convictions and remain focused. If someone is draining your time and energy, it may be time to move away from them. You could even recommend them to your competition to help everyone find better fits.

Remember, you can't be everything to everyone; trying to do so will only lead to frustration and stagnation. Invest in self-development courses to learn how to effectively say no—it will ultimately help your business thrive in the long run and help you become unstuck.

To overcome fears about my weaknesses, I created **Weekly Self-Assessment Exercises** to help me identify and track my weaknesses in a structured way. It's short, practical, and designed for busy business owners like yourself.

Weekly Self-Assessment Exercises

Leadership & Decision-Making

- Did I make decisions quickly, based on data and input, or did I delay?

- Was I confident in my choices, or did I second-guess myself too often?

- Did I clearly communicate my decisions to my team?

Weakness signals: indecisiveness, lack of clarity, micromanaging.

<u>Time & Focus</u>

- How much of my week was spent on strategic vs. operational tasks?

- Did I delegate effectively, or did I handle tasks someone else could do?

- Did I stick to priorities, or get distracted by low-value activities?

Weakness signals: poor delegation, firefighting, and lack of focus.

<u>Financial Oversight</u>

- Do I understand my current cash flow position?

- Did I review key financial accounts (income statement, balance sheet, etc.)?

- Did I make financial decisions proactively or reactively?

Weakness signals: poor financial report understanding, neglecting numbers, and overspending.

<u>Customer & Market</u>

- Did I spend time talking to or listening to customers this week?

- Did I track customer satisfaction (complaints, referrals)?

- Did I review competitor or market trends?

Weakness signals: losing touch with customers, ignoring feedback, lagging behind competition.

<u>Team & Culture</u>

- Did I motivate or inspire my team this week?

- Did I give constructive feedback and recognise good work?

- Did I address conflicts or performance issues promptly?

Weakness signals: low morale, unclear roles, poor communication.

<u>Personal Growth & Energy</u>

- Did I invest in learning (reading, training, mentorship)?

- Was my energy level high, or did I feel drained most of the week?

- Did I manage stress in healthy ways (exercise, rest, routines)?

Weakness signals: burnout, stagnation, lack of self-care.

Scoring & Tracking

- **Score each area 1–5** (1 = very weak, 5 = strong).

- **Highlight the lowest-scoring areas** each week.

- Pick *1 weakness* to actively work on in the next 7 days.

- Track trends over time—how are scores changing?

Remember to focus on your strengths while also keeping an eye on areas that need improvement. By shifting your mindset from doubt to opportunity, you'll not only enhance your business but also foster a more positive environment for yourself and your team. Let's embrace the challenge of turning weaknesses into strengths and building a brighter, more innovative future together! Keep pushing forward—you have the skills and creativity to make an impact!

Chapter 6
Reignite Energy

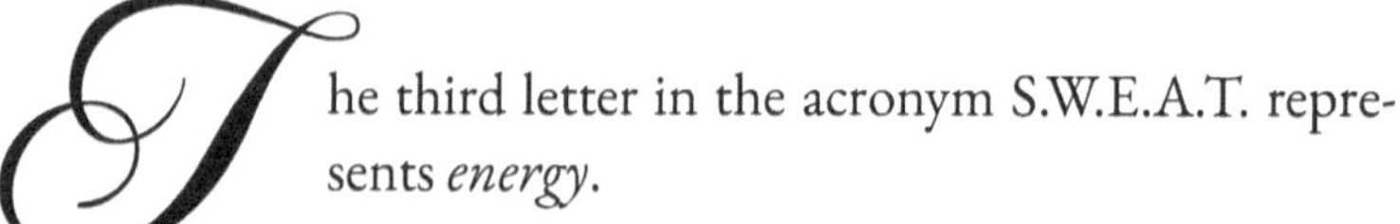

The third letter in the acronym S.W.E.A.T. represents *energy*.

Every business owner begins with a spark: it might be the thrill of solving a problem, the ambition to create a legacy, or simply the desire for freedom. This energy is a blend of passion, creativity, and perseverance. Yet as many seasoned business owners know, maintaining this energy is easier said than done over time in a business.

At some point, nearly every business owner finds themselves stuck: revenue stalls, inspiration fades, teams disengage, and the joy of building something meaningful becomes more centred on the grind of simply keeping the lights on. This is not failure, but a sign that the business or perhaps the business owner needs a recalibration.

This chapter explores what business owner energy really means, why it fades, and, more importantly, how to restore it, whether you've hit a plateau and your growth feels burned out or you just can't seem to get your mojo back. You'll find practical exercises, mindset shifts, and renewed inspiration to reignite your inner fire and push your business forward.

What is Energy for a Business Owner?

Energy is the fuel that powers vision, action, and resilience in business. It encompasses 4 types of energy, such as:

Creative Energy

This is the drive to solve problems, innovate, and think outside the box. When you need to pivot to a new product, service, or to restart your business, tapping into your creativity is essential. It allows you to brainstorm innovative ways to attract new customers or enhance what you offer to existing ones, ultimately generating more revenue. Below are some exercises to help ignite your creative energy.

The Brainstorming Exercise

What's one business challenge you'd like to explore today (e.g., attracting more clients, improving customer loyalty, boosting revenue, standing out from competitors, etc.)?

Set a Bold Constraint. Imagine a radical limitation or rule on your business. For example:

"I can't spend any money on marketing."

"I only have one hour a week to work on this."

"I must sell my product (or service) without using words, i.e., use photos, videos, or infographics to show the *benefits* instead of describing them in text."

Brainstorm Without Judgment. For 10 minutes, list as many wild ideas as possible under that constraint. Don't filter or critique. The stranger, the better.

Switch Perspective Ask: "How would a child, a famous innovator, or even my biggest competitor solve this?" Write down answers.

Extract Practical Insights Review your list. Circle any ideas that could realistically be adapted or spark a fresh direction.

Why This is Effective:

– Constraints **force creativity** by breaking routine thinking.

– Switching perspectives **broadens imagination** beyond your own biases.

– Reviewing and adapting ensures you **capture usable business insights**.

Emotional Energy

Creative energy sparks ideas, but **emotional energy** fuels resilience, connection, and leadership—critical for business owners. This involves the passion and emotional resilience required to navigate the ups and downs of business ownership. Your emotional energy will propel you forward, helping you to view obstacles as challenges rather than threats.

Here's an exercise designed to tap into that:

The "Emotional Fuel to Strategy" Exercise

Purpose: Convert your emotions (positive or negative) into momentum for business growth.

Name the Emotion

Take 2 minutes and write down what you're *really* feeling about your business right now. Such as:

"I feel frustrated about slow sales."

"I feel excited about a new opportunity."

"I feel anxious about cash flow."

Locate the Sources

Ask: *"Where is this emotion coming from?"*

Is it tied to unmet expectations?

A recent win?

A fear about the future?

A sense of pride in progress?

Flip it into Energy

For negative emotions:

Frustration → "What system is broken, and how can I fix it?"

Fear → "What would I do if I trusted myself fully?"

Anger → "What boundary do I need to set?"

For positive emotions:

Excitement → "What bold move can I make to amplify this?"

Gratitude → "Who can I thank or reward today?"

Channel It into an Action

Decide on **1 concrete business action** tied to that emotion. Some examples are:

- If frustrated with marketing, commit to testing one new marketing channel this week. Examples of marketing channels are:

- Social media: Great for visibility, brand awareness, and building a community such as Facebook, Instagram, or YouTube.

- Search-based: Customers find you through Google ads and online local business directories when looking for what you offer.

- Content marketing to educate or inspire, such as blog posts, YouTube tutorials, guides, and e-Books.

- Email and messaging: Great for follow-ups and repeat business, for example, email newsletters, automated email responders, and Facebook Messenger marketing.

- Marketplace channels for product-based businesses such as Amazon, eBay, and Shopify.

The channels used will depend on the best channels for your business industry. These are just a few; however, the marketing channels that you own and control are your website, email list, and blog posts.

– If excited about a new client → capture that story as a case study to research and share with your customers/clients.

– If anxious about money → review cash flow projections today.

Anchor the Energy

Before you close the exercise, take a deep breath and say: *"I can use my emotions as fuel, not weight."* This reinforces that emotions aren't distractions—they're signals for strategy.

Why This Is Effective:

This is effective because business owners often try to **suppress** emotions to "stay professional." Instead, by reframing, you turn emotional energy into focus and momentum.

Physical Energy

This refers to the stamina necessary to handle long days, significant challenges, and competing priorities. It's important to maintain your physical energy and capabilities to stay energised and consistent in pursuing your goals.

Here's a **simple 5-minute daily physical energy routine** designed for business owners. It wakes up your body, sharpens your mind, and ties the boost directly to business focus. Consult your doctor if you are unsure if this routine is effective for you.

Five-Minute "Business Energy Reset" Routine

Minute 1 – Breath & Grounding

Stand tall, feet shoulder-width apart.

Inhale deeply through your nose (4 seconds), hold (2 seconds), exhale through your mouth (6 seconds).

Repeat 3–4 cycles. Affirm silently: *"I am charging my body to power my business."*

Minutes 2–3 – Power Moves

Do a short burst of physical activity—enough to elevate your heart rate and oxygen flow.

Key: **no phone, no distractions.** Just movement + breathing.

Minute 4 – Stretch & Open

– Raise arms wide and stretch chest open (expands confidence).

– Twist gently side to side (releases tension).

– Roll shoulders back slowly (posture reset for presence).

Minute 5 – Business Focus Prompt

While standing tall and breathing deeply, ask yourself:

- *"What's the one action today that will move my business forward the most?"* Write it down immediately in a notebook as a journal entry.

Why This Is Effective:

- **Movement** unlocks blood flow and hormones (dopamine, serotonin) that boost creativity.

- **Writing after moving** taps into clarity, not overthinking.

- **Immediate action** builds momentum, turning physical energy into business energy.

By the end, you've **moved, centred, and connected in a body-to-business strategy**. Do it at the start of the day, or anytime you hit a slump.

Mental Energy

If **creative energy** sparks ideas, **emotional energy** drives resilience, and **physical energy** fuels stamina—then **mental energy** is all about focus, clarity, and decision-making. All these types of energy are interconnected. Business owners often waste their mental energy on distractions, overthinking, or "firefighting" problems. Mental energy is essential for maintaining the focus required to make quick decisions that can alter the direction of your business.

Here's an exercise to harness and direct your mental energy:

The "Mental Energy Allocation" Exercise

Purpose: Protect your best brainpower for high-value business decisions instead of draining it on low-value tasks.

Step 1. Daily Brain Dump (5 minutes)

- Write down everything on your mind: tasks, worries, ideas, to-dos.

- Don't organise yet—just empty your head onto paper.

Step 2. Sort by Energy Value

Make 2 columns:

- **High-Mental-Energy Tasks** → strategy, decision-making, creative planning, negotiation.

- **Low-Mental-Energy Tasks** → email-sorting, admin, routine processes.

Step 3. Time Block Your Peak Energy

- Ask yourself: *"When do I feel mentally sharpest—morning, afternoon, or evening?"*

- Schedule **high-value tasks ONLY** in that window.

- Push low-energy tasks to off-peak times or delegate them.

Step 4. Set a "Mental Sprint" (25 minutes)

- Pick ONE high-value task.

- Set a timer for 25 minutes.

- During this time, you focus only on that task.

- Take a 5-minute break.

- During this time, you focus only on that task.

- No distractions—checking email, no switching tabs, no multitasking——just deep focus.

- Take a 5-minute break (stand up, stretch, breathe).

Step 5. Protect & Recharge

Before shifting tasks, ask:

"Did I just spend my best mental energy on what moves the business forward?" If yes → celebrate. If no → adjust tomorrow's focus.

Why This is Effective:

- Clears mental clutter (less stress).

- Prevents wasting peak brainpower on low-level tasks.

- Builds a habit of **mental discipline → business momentum.**

Reigniting Energy

To ignite your business spirit once again, let's start by reconnecting with your "why." Reflecting on the purpose that initially fuelled your passion for your business is one of the most effective ways to re-energise your journey. So, grab a pen and some paper or dust off that old journal, and let's dive into these enlightening questions together:

<u>What inspired me to start this business?</u> Remember the spark that propelled you into this adventure. Everyone's journey is different, and your unique motivation is what sets you apart. Think about what truly inspired you to take that leap of faith. What dreams were you chasing at that time?

<u>What problem do I genuinely care about solving?</u> Standing out in your field is essential, and your passion for the solution you offer plays a huge role in this answer. Customers often make purchases for either enjoyment or to alleviate their challenges. Reflect on the specific issue you're passionate about tackling

and the number of individuals you're impacting through your business.

<u>Who am I aiming to help?</u> If you've been feeling stagnant, it might be time to reassess your target market. Visualise your ideal customer or client. What insights or feedback have you gained? Which demographics are truly contributing to your success? Take, for example, from chapter 1, David, who initially focused his sustainable furniture business on eco-conscious consumers. He discovered that many potential clients preferred thrift-store shopping for their sustainability needs. By pivoting his business to attract this audience, his business flourished remarkably!

As you ponder these questions, keep in mind that circumstances might have evolved, and there could be fresh opportunities waiting for you to uncover. Do some research within your niche to identify emerging trends you can integrate into your business. These reflections are vital for recalibrating your focus. Consider crafting a personal mission statement that includes your purpose and placing it somewhere prominent. This will serve as a daily reminder of why you started your business and help guide your decisions while filtering out distractions.

Embrace this opportunity for self-discovery and watch as the energy flows back into your business and personal pursuits!

For an example of business-owner energy, consider Steve Irwin (1962-2006), the legendary Australian "Crocodile Hunter" and founder of Australia Zoo. His story was one of a passion-driven business and is a powerful example of someone who developed incredible energy to grow a business from humble beginnings.

Steve Irwin didn't just build a zoo—he built a global wildlife movement. Born into a family of wildlife lovers, Steve took over his parents' small reptile park in Queensland in the early 1990s and transformed it into the Australia Zoo, now one of the most famous conservation centres in the world.

But in the beginning, the zoo was just a struggling roadside wildlife park with limited visitors and low income. Steve often had to live modestly and work long hours, doing everything from feeding crocodiles to cleaning enclosures himself (https://biographics.org/steve-irwin-biography-wildlife-conservationist/).

How Steve Irwin Developed the Energy to Keep Going

Unshakable Passion for Wildlife: Steve loved animals—especially reptiles—with every fibre of his being; that passion created natural energy. Even when exhausted, he would light up when working with animals or teaching others about them.

Turned Purpose into Power: His deeper mission was conservation. He wasn't just running a zoo; he wanted to save endangered species and change how the world saw wildlife. That clear "why" gave him relentless drive.

Used Media to Energise the Mission: Instead of relying solely on ticket sales, he began filming documentaries. His show, *The Crocodile Hunter*, became a global hit. The attention helped fund the zoo, expand conservation efforts, and energised Steve to keep growing his vision.

Thrived on Action: Steve had a hands-on personality. He didn't sit in offices—he wrestled crocs, rescued snakes, and travelled the world. Physical movement and excitement were part of how he created energy, not lost it.

Support from His Family: His wife, Terri, was his business and life partner. Together, they pushed through financial stress, public pressure, and long days. That deep family bond was fuel during the tough times.

Steve Irwin said, "If you can't find joy in what you're doing, you'll never have the strength to keep going. I wake up every morning and can't wait to get to work."

Even after his passing in 2006, his legacy thrives—with Australia Zoo expanding and his family continuing his mission. Steve Irwin was a true example of how energy comes from passion, purpose, and living fully into your mission.

Take a moment to examine what is draining your energy. Identify the people and habits that deplete your motivation. Common culprits can include micromanaging your team if you have employees, failing to set boundaries with clients, and saying yes when you should be saying no to new business opportunities that don't align with your objectives. Are there particular clients who drain your energy and make it difficult for you to work with them? It's important to recognise this, as dealing with energy-draining relationships prevents you from performing at your best. Sometimes, it's best to part ways.

Consider how exhausting it would be to run a business where everyone is sapping your energy. Relationships with clients are built on trust, effective communication, and getting things done. Some clients may not deliver that, and while I don't advocate for dropping customers lightly, if they are exhausting you, it raises the question of whether the partnership is truly worthwhile.

Before taking on a new client, spend some time getting to know them and their expectations. Ask about their needs and challenges to determine if there is a mutual fit.

Lack of sleep or exercise and spending too much time on day-to-day operations rather than strategic thinking can also drain your energy. As a business owner, it's important to recognise that you can't do everything. Consider outsourcing certain tasks, either to an external business or by hiring an employee or contractor.

For example, when it comes to bookkeeping, many start with a simple Excel spreadsheet, which is acceptable for a time. However, you don't want to spend all your time on bookkeeping at the expense of business opportunities. Thankfully, there are excellent software solutions available now that can transform bookkeeping functions (as mentioned earlier). Many external services offer bookkeeping through such software, which you can subscribe to. This way, you can outsource the bookkeeping tasks while maintaining control over the software, allowing you to run important reports without the extra time.

The financial reports produced are essential for monitoring the health of your business, so by outsourcing daily transactional entries, you free up your time to manage your business more effectively and avoid letting the business manage you.

Revisit your vision regularly to tap into all these energies inside you. Your original goals may be outdated, or you may have outgrown your initial vision and need to dream bigger. Take out your journal and write down your ideal business vision for 5 years from now. Be specific about your revenue, team, lifestyle, and impact. What steps do you need to take to reach this vision?

By updating your vision, you can shift your mindset towards curiosity and momentum. Perhaps it's time to reignite your vision or introduce a new service or product.

Practical Exercises for Re-energising

You may recall from chapter 2 that I mentioned the 80/20 rule, also known as the Pareto Principle, which states that 20% of your clients generate 80% of your revenue. This principle can also be applied to your tasks: 20% of your tasks yield 80% of your joy or results.

To reduce overwhelm and increase satisfaction, focus on high-leverage activities. Consider outsourcing low-level tasks that consume your time and energy to employees or contractors. You don't want to spend your valuable time on tasks that can easily be delegated or outsourced.

Designing Your CEO Schedule

Create a weekly routine that aligns with your highest priorities. Make sure to include time for visioning—set aside 1 to 2 hours per week for this. Visioning is a crucial strategy, as it provides you with a clear path toward achieving your goals for the present and future. Visualising your success can also evoke the emotions associated with reaching those goals.

If you have employees, dedicate time for delegation and team meetings. Spend time on activities that drive revenue, such as sales and marketing. Additionally, make sure to allocate time for unstructured creative thinking. This is your opportunity to step back from everyday tasks and focus on the bigger picture.

Sometimes, taking a retreat gives us the space to think more clearly. Consider booking a retreat, either alone or with friends, to reflect on what is working and what isn't in your business. You can revisit your goals, explore journaling, or meditate. Stepping away from your usual environment often leads to breakthroughs, as if you're stepping outside to gain a different perspective. Silence, from the usual noises in your life, is incredibly powerful and can provide answers. It's remarkable how, in those quiet moments, ideas can flow to you.

Embrace Identity Shift

Who you were when you started your business isn't necessarily who you need to be now. Transitioning from a builder to a leader, from a doer to a delegator, and from reactive to proactive can take energy. Growth requires an evolution of your identity, so acknowledge the old version of yourself and consciously choose to embrace a new one.

Adopt a Growth Mindset

See challenges as opportunities instead of viewing them as defeats. Reflect on the resilience you develop through overcoming obstacles (as we shared earlier). Instead of seeing challenges as failures, ask yourself what you can learn from each situation and what implementations you need to consider, what energy to use. Challenges may require you to pivot, but they also present opportunities. Energy flows where attention goes, so focus your attention on future potential rather than current problems.

Renewing Physical and Emotional Energy

You can't pour from an empty cup, so prioritise the following:

Sleep: This is non-negotiable. Aim for 7 to 8 hours each night.

Nutrition: Fuel your brain and body with whole foods.

Exercise: Aim for at least 20 minutes of movement each day to help clear your mind.

Hydration: Prevent dehydration, which can mimic fatigue. What feels like exhaustion might just be your body crying out for hydration. Drink up and feel the difference!

Nature: Spending time in nature boosts serotonin and creativity.

Your business runs more effectively when your body does. You don't need to tackle significant physical challenges every day; consistency is key. Start with small daily activities, such as an early morning walk, meditation, or simply taking time to relax before starting your day. Waking up early helps develop discipline—approach it consistently, even in small increments. Start your day with intention, energy, and drive, and the rest of the day will follow suit. Even small habits, like making your bed every morning, are habits of discipline that kickstart your day.

Focus on movement, meditation, or just quiet time to feel the energy flow through your body. Recognising and nurturing these sources of energy, including adequate sleep, is crucial for sustained growth and productivity.

We need these daily energy rituals, so in the morning, have a gratitude journaling. It's amazing how you feel once you think of the things around you that you have gratitude for; even just facing another day. When you have thoughts and ideas, write them in your journal. Don't put them on scraps of paper; it's great to look back and reference. Don't just keep it in your head; it's amazing how there are so many other things you just forget or just can't remember the exact terminology or recall how you felt when you wrote it down, so journaling is very important.

Reinvention

Reinventing your business can take many forms: it might involve exploring a new niche, launching an innovative product, or enhancing a service you already offer. Alternatively, it could mean refining your operations, elevating your marketing strategies, or enriching the overall customer experience. Whatever path you choose, it's essential to give yourself the freedom to experiment.

Today's buyers want more personalisation, speed, and values (like sustainability). Reinventing helps you stay aligned with what your customers in your particular market truly care about.

Let's summarise what we've discussed in this chapter by applying the "**7 Techniques to Build Energy.**"

1. Reconnect with Your "Why"

Energy without direction is just noise.

Revisit why you started your business.

Write a short purpose/mission statement and read it daily.

Ask: "Who am I helping? Why does this matter beyond money?"

2. Daily Movement to Shake Off Stagnation

Motion creates emotion.

Even 15 minutes of walking, stretching, or exercise boosts dopamine and clarity.

Schedule it as a non-negotiable part of your day.

Try "walk-and-think" sessions to generate ideas and relieve stress.

3. Micro-Wins and Celebration Rituals

Small wins compound into momentum.

Write down one win each day—no matter how small.

Celebrate with something joyful (music, a fist pump, a 2-minute dance break).

Keeps your brain focused on progress, not just pressure.

4. Energy Check-In: People, Tasks, Environments

Some things drain you; others energise you. Know the difference.

Ask weekly:

Which tasks energise me?

Which people give me strength?

Which environments inspire me?

Then increase exposure to energisers, reduce exposure to drainers.

5. Time-Boxed Breaks & Digital Detox

A *time-boxed break* means you deliberately set a fixed time for rest or pause during work (like 5, 10, or 15 minutes).

A digital detox is time where you *intentionally disconnect* from phones, email, social media, and screens.

You can't hustle from an empty tank.

Use the Pomodoro technique: 25 min. work / 5 min. rest.

Take one day per week to not think about the business.

Block off "white space" in your calendar—time to breathe and refocus.

Take midday walk breaks, get some sunlight, and step away from the computer.

6. Visual Reminders of Vision

Make the dream visible.

Create a "vision board" or poster of your goal, customers, and why you started.

Keep it on your wall or desktop to keep in view.

When energy drops, look up instead of looking down.

7. Outsource Tasks

External services will help with bookkeeping.

Create space for yourself to focus on strategic decision-making.

Effective communication is paramount, and you don't want to be overwhelmed by mundane tasks that distract you from what truly matters. Explore automation options for routine tasks—like filtering and managing emails—to save time and ensure prompt responses to client inquiries. Implementing these scalable systems not only frees up your valuable time but also clears your mental space, allowing for greater creativity and focus.

Injecting fresh innovation into your business is vital; stagnation often stems from repetitive routines. Embrace the opportunity to research and test new products or services, launch engaging challenges or campaigns, and consider collaborating with partners outside your industry. Engaging with your community and fostering collaboration can create a dynamic environment ripe for growth. Join a mastermind group or a networking club—these communities can provide you with invaluable resources. You'll gain new perspectives, share wisdom, and enjoy the encouragement that comes from surrounding yourself with ambitious small business owners who can reignite your passion.

Additionally, engaging a coach or advisor might be precisely what you need. Sometimes, having a sounding board can provide clarity. Business coaches can provide guidance, mindset coaches can help you overcome mental blocks, and financial advisors can guide you in optimising your resources. Remember, the business journey need not be a solo venture.

Finally, mentoring others can be a rewarding way to rejuvenate your energy. Share your expertise by speaking at events, mentoring young business owners, or documenting your journey through a podcast. Teaching not only enriches others but also reconnects you with your purpose and passion for your business, reviving the enthusiasm that first drove you to start your business.

Conclusion:

Being stuck is a turning point, a signal to reflect, realign, and recharge. Business energy isn't about hustle 24/7. It's about clarity of purpose, alignment with your values, smart strategy, and sustainable execution. By reconnecting with your vision, honouring your health, cultivating your mindset, and surrounding yourself with the right people, you can transform stagnation into momentum.

So, if you're feeling stuck—good, it means you care. It means you've come far enough to know something's off. Now, it's time to re-ignite that flame. Your next breakthrough is closer than you think.

> "Crikey! Life's too short not to give it everything you've got." – Steve Irwin

Chapter 7
Call to Action

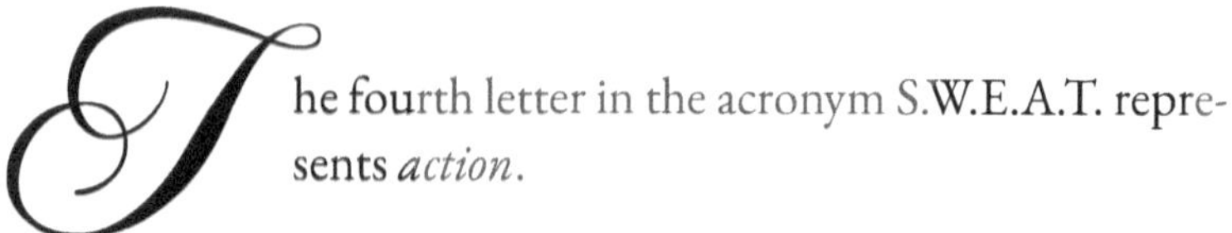

The fourth letter in the acronym S.W.E.A.T. represents *action*.

"Everything that exists in your life does so because of two things: something you did or something you didn't do." - Albert Einstein

Owning and running a business is a journey fuelled by dreams but powered by taking action. Many people have big ideas, grand visions, and powerful motivations—but what separates the successful business owner from the one who stays stuck is a simple truth: **Action beats inaction every time**.

Too many business owners find themselves not growing—by fear, overthinking, or waiting for the "perfect" moment (as I shared earlier). They get stuck in planning, stuck in doubt, stuck in comparison. But success does not come to the most prepared or the most talented—it comes to those who *move*, those who *try*, those who *take imperfect action*, and learn as they go.

This chapter explains why consistent, focused action is essential for business growth and how to avoid common pitfalls that keep business owners stuck.

Melanie Perkins – Co-Founder of Canva

Melanie Perkins, a University student from Australia, had an idea to make graphic design simple for everyone. She and her co-founder faced over 100 investor rejections while pitching Canva. Rather than give up, she kept refining the pitch, learning from feedback, and taking small steps to build the platform piece by piece (*Melanie Perkins: The Canva Story: The Compendious Biography of an Australian Female Tech Entrepreneur, a Tech Pioneer, and The Founder of Canva. 2024*).

Action Taken: Persistently pitched her idea to investors despite 100s of rejections.

Result: Canva became a multi-billion-dollar company with over 100,000,000 users worldwide—and Melanie became one of the youngest female tech CEOs in the world.

Melanie succeeded because she **took bold action**—not because she had everything figured out. Her story is proof that taking action beats excuses, and progress starts with one step forward.

One day, as I was heading into the city for a meetings, I saw a building with the phrase "Knowledge is Power" in big, bold letters for everyone to see. However, I disagree with that statement. Knowledge alone isn't power unless it is put into action. Many intelligent people find themselves unhappy because they do not act on what they know. There are numerous business owners with excellent knowledge and experience who feel stuck because they haven't taken the necessary steps to apply their knowledge.

Action is what truly serves as power. You can possess a vast amount of information, but if you don't act on it, you won't make any progress. It's essential to apply the knowledge you have, as this builds momentum, and you gain it by consistently taking action each day.

"The best way to predict the future is to create it." – Peter Drucker

This quote reminds business owners that **growth doesn't come by waiting—it comes by doing**. Taking intentional, forward-moving action—even small steps—builds the future you want.

Many people hesitate to take action in business because they are waiting for the perfect moment or believe they need to be fully prepared. However, this approach is ineffective; you will never feel completely ready and will only end up postponing what needs to be done. Time is of the essence. The sooner you act, the sooner you gain momentum. Even if your actions don't provide you with the results you expected, at least you took a step forward, and you can learn from the outcome, whether good or bad.

Comfort Zone

"A comfort zone is a beautiful place, but nothing ever grows there." – Unknown

It's true that growth comes from taking action, witnessing the results, and gaining momentum to take more action. However, some people choose not to take action because they don't feel confident enough to move forward. They feel stuck and negotiate with themselves about why now isn't the right time or wait for someone else to take the lead. These excuses keep piling up, and, eventually, they retreat back to their comfort zone, where it feels safe.

In your comfort zone, you do things that you are familiar with that give you peace. While it's important to have relaxation in your life, success doesn't come from remaining peaceful and relaxed all the time. If you aspire to be a successful business owner, you need to take action that can move you forward, involving creating a plan for what needs to be accomplished and following through.

Avoid making excuses or getting distracted by chores, shopping, or social media. Distraction is the opposite of discipline. Discipline is making yourself do something even when you don't feel like it; distractions, on the other hand, only push back the time you need to focus on your goals. If you truly need to put something into action, you should block out an hour each day without distractions. This hour should be dedicated to your thoughts and to working on what needs to be done in your business to help it grow. It's crucial not to let distractions interfere with your progress.

You may feel stuck because you're not experiencing growth, one sign of being stagnant; you might not feel as fulfilled as you once did in this state. To overcome this, it's important to pivot and introduce something new into your business that sparks your excitement.

As an Australian CPA, I spent 25 years supporting small business owners as their accountant and realised many were struggling with far more than their finances. Determined to help them move forward, and with no prior experience, I became a motivational self-help author focused on guiding small business owners who feel stuck in their businesses. This is something new that I introduced into the business that excites me. I knew I had more to offer a broader customer base and to support self-development. Determined to help small business owners move forward and grow, I wrote this book to inspire them to keep going, keep building, and keep believing in their dreams and vision.

Consider doing some research in areas where you feel less confident to help improve your skills. Gaining momentum is crucial, and the best way to achieve that is to take one step forward.

"A journey of 1,000 miles begins with one step." –
Lao Tzu

Taking steps towards your goals can start with small actions; they don't have to be giant leaps. If you attempt a giant step, it can be challenging to maintain momentum. Life often gets in the way, and this can lead to feeling disheartened when you can't keep going. The idea is to start with small steps that build your confidence.

However, don't let the need to feel competent stop you from taking action. Waiting to feel fully prepared can be counterproductive, as you need to act in order to gain confidence, which will grow the more you engage in the tasks you want to accomplish. As you take action, you will develop more confidence in yourself, which will encourage you to innovate and create.

Fear can creep in, telling you that you aren't good enough or experienced enough to make that phone call, post that blog, or record that podcast. However, it's important to push those fears aside. The only way to improve is to start and learn as you go.

Procrastination

Remember, the most successful business owners didn't begin as experts; they started as beginners and progressed over time. What set them apart was their ability to take consistent action. Another misconception of success is that people can't act unless they're motivated. which is often an excuse. Once you start taking action, motivation tends to follow, and momentum builds. It's incredible how much weight we place on tasks, both in business and personal life, which often leads to procrastination.

We create excuses, feel uncomfortable, and postpone tasks until we feel ready or until we have more time or fewer distractions. However, that ideal situation rarely occurs (as shared in the section before). Remember, you only have so many hours in a day. Make it purposeful. Once you start, you'll be amazed at how the mountain you thought you created isn't as big as you imagined. You'll actually begin to enjoy the process.

So, don't overthink what needs to be done before taking the necessary actions to move from being stuck to getting unstuck. The real problem often lies in not taking that initial step. You already know what needs to be done—you know who you need to talk to or how to approach them.

If you feel discouraged, don't give up. Keep pursuing your passion. Remember your "why"—the reason you started your business in the first place. Revisit your vision and your journals; these are essential tools that can help you. Reflect on what you wrote in your journal about your vision. Imagine where you want to be in your business in 5 years. Think about how good it will feel to know that the effort you put in has led you to where you are now, while you continue to grow.

Some people give up too early and fail to realise what awaits them on the other side. Don't waste your time, effort, and energy by walking away. If this is truly what you want and why you started your business, don't let the feeling of being stuck deter you. Don't allow your inner voice to tell you that you're not good enough because you are. You're good enough to start, so you are good enough to continue.

Make the most of each day. Wake up early, embrace the day, and practice gratitude for where you are and for the wonderful people around you. You'll be surprised at how much energy you can develop from a positive mindset rather than waking up focused on what needs to be done or being distracted by procrastination.

10 Procrastination-Busting Techniques

1. The 5-Minute Start Rule

"Just start for five minutes."

Commit to working on a task for just five minutes. Once you begin, momentum often takes over. Starting is the hardest part—not continuing is easy.

2. Break It Down to Micro-Tasks

Big tasks = overwhelm. Small tasks = doable = progress

Instead of "Launch website," write:

Choose a domain name.

Write homepage headline.

Add a contact form.

3. Set "Pain-Free" Deadlines

Self-imposed deadlines reduce avoidance.

Create short, friendly deadlines with a reward (e.g., "Finish this by 3 p.m., then take a coffee break"). Use timers or calendar blocks to create structure.

4. Use the "2-Minute Rule"

"If an action takes less than two minutes, it should be done at the moment it's defined." – David Allen

Perfect for emails, replies, and tiny admin tasks that clutter your brain. Clears mental space fast.

Writing down, organising, and revisiting tiny tasks takes longer than just doing them.

5. Batch Similar Tasks Together

Switching tasks burns energy. Grouping builds flow.

Do all creative tasks in one block. Admin in another, sales calls in one hour. Your brain works better this way.

6. Remove Temptations & Triggers

Procrastination is often just a distraction away.

Silence your phone.

7. Use Visual Progress Tools

Progress = motivation.

Use checklists, Kanban boards, or habit trackers. Watching progress builds momentum.

8. Tie Tasks to Your Vision

"Why does this task matter to the mission?"

If something feels boring or draining, reconnect it to the impact:

"This email = potential client."

"This ad = someone gets helped."

9. Accountability = Action

Tell someone your goal for the day.

Find an accountability partner, group, or coach. Share your top 1–3 daily tasks and report progress. External accountability beats inner excuses.

10. Forgive

If you slip, don't spiral.

Procrastination is human. Don't beat yourself up. Just restart. Ask:

"What's the smallest step I can take right now?"

> "Be not afraid of going slowly, be afraid only of standing still." – Chinese Proverb

Do it "Right Now"

Rise early, feel great, and progress through the day. If you need to do something, do it *"right now."* If you need to make that call, tell yourself to do it *"right now."* This way, you won't allow your inner voice to negotiate with you, saying to do it later. Later might never come, and then you'll feel drained instead of energised.

Put a little reminder around you to act *"right now."* Don't overthink how others might respond to your podcast or anything you share. People aren't looking for polished presentations; they are looking for authenticity. Create emotion and tell stories—they resonate with people and make you relatable.

When you speak, be comfortable and be yourself. Remember, you're unique—there's only one of you. Don't try to mimic your competition; instead, present yourself genuinely. You can't change things unless you're actively engaged. Mistakes will happen, but that's part of learning. Everyone makes mistakes, so don't be too hard on yourself if something doesn't work the first time, or at all.

Keep moving forward; life and business are learning curves. Don't sit around feeling sorry for yourself. Get out there—people need what you're offering. They need your product or service to solve their problems. If you don't show up, who will? There's enough opportunity for *everyone*, so don't be distracted by your competition. Focus on being yourself and remember that forming genuine relationships with your customers and clients will make them want to see you.

"An ongoing relationship with customers is a great
thing from a business point of view." – Bill Gates

When we started our tricycle business, we initially began with
2-wheeled bikes because that's what we rode, and we liked the
idea of electric bikes. They propelled you to where you wanted
to go without making you sweaty, allowing you to ride to work,
get changed, and feel great. I experienced this first-hand; riding
to work every day was an excellent way to start my day.

Listen to the Market

As I mentioned earlier, when my husband and I began marketing
our bikes, people began asking us, "Why don't you sell tricycles?"
At first, we were puzzled; I associated tricycles with kids and
didn't see the potential. But when a friend of my mother suggested it again, we thought, *Why not?* We decided to get a couple
of samples and put them out there. We took action, did some
research, and when the tricycles arrived, they sold immediately.
We soon realised we were onto something.

What we didn't initially realise was that the big retailers were
getting truckloads of 2-wheeled electric bicycles and saturating
the market. We wanted to pivot and present something different.
There were very few players catering to customers with balancing issues who still wanted to spend time outdoors. The oldest
person we sold to was a 90-year-old man who loved his tricycle
so much that he bought one for his wife (as I stated earlier in the
book).

Our tricycles didn't require much physical exertion; you could
put in as little or as much effort as you wanted. This made it
easier for seniors to enjoy fresh air and exercise without worrying
about balancing issues. We had even adjusted the design so that

you could lean into corners without tilting, which was an added advantage.

It was only through taking action and listening to the market that we succeeded in this endeavour. We could have held our ground and tried to compete with the big players, but we adapted. When COVID-19 hit, we wanted to sell our business but discovered that outdoor activity was still allowed in Australia, so instead, we focused on selling all our stock. There was significant demand for our tricycles during that time. Who would have thought? We ended up selling everything we had instead of selling the business. We finished on a high note, glad to know how many people we helped during such a challenging and unprecedented period.

This experience taught us the importance of listening to the market. If you ever feel stuck, I encourage you to talk to people in your industry. Get out of your space and engage with them about their challenges and needs.

Experience the difference: What sets the extraordinary apart from the ordinary is how you act in moments when you don't feel like doing anything at all. How many times have you told yourself, "I'll start tomorrow"? How many dreams have you put on hold because you weren't in the mood? How many opportunities have slipped away while you waited for the right moment? You need to change your daily habits if you find yourself stuck because the ones you currently have may not be helping you progress. Maybe it's a habit we pick up occasionally, but it needs to become a daily practice. Even brushing your teeth is a daily habit.

Most people have it backward; they think action follows motivation. They believe they need to feel good to start working, but here's the revolutionary truth: Action creates motivation. Motion creates emotion. The very act of doing something generates the energy to keep doing it.

Think about the last time you procrastinated on a task. Procrastination is choosing to do something easy or comfortable now instead of what truly needs to be done. Remember how it loomed over you like a dark cloud? Your mind magnified its difficulty. But when you finally started, what happened? Suddenly, it wasn't so terrible. The momentum kicked in, the energy followed, and the cloud lifted. This isn't just philosophy; it's biology. Your brain is wired to conserve energy, programmed to seek comfort and avoid discomfort.

This understanding made perfect sense when we were hunting for food and running from predators, but in today's world, this ancient programming is sabotaging your success. Every time you force yourself to work when you don't feel like it, you're rewiring your brain. You're building new neural pathways and developing what I call "success muscles." Just like physical muscles, these mental muscles grow stronger with each repetition and each moment of discomfort you push through.

This step isn't easy; if it were, everyone would be living their dreams. The path of least resistance is always available and tempting. That's why average is so common while excellence is rare. It demands something most people aren't willing to give – consistent action, regardless of feelings.

> "If you want something you have never had, you must be willing to do something you have never done." – Thomas Jefferson

People transform their lives using this simple but powerful principle. A single mother who wrote her book by waking up 2 hours early every day, even though she was exhausted. A middle-aged man who built a successful business by making 50 cold calls daily, even though he hated every minute of it. A middle-aged dad who lost 27 kgs (60 lbs) by hitting the gym at 5:00 a.m., even though his bed begged him to stay.

These people weren't special, blessed with extraordinary willpower or superhuman motivation. They simply understood one crucial truth: Feelings are fickle, but actions are absolute. They learned to treat their important tasks like breathing—non-negotiable regardless of mood.

Here's a secret that successful people know: Procrastination is not a time-management problem but a pain-management problem. We don't avoid tasks because we're lazy; we avoid them because we're trying to escape discomfort. But what if I told you that this discomfort is actually a compass? What if the very thing you're avoiding is exactly what you should be doing? The tasks that make you uncomfortable are usually the ones that matter most, leading to growth, breakthroughs, and transformation. The business presentation you're nervous about could lead to new clients. The conversation you're avoiding could save a relationship. The workout you're dreading could add years to your life.

When you understand this truth, everything changes. Suddenly, discomfort becomes a signal, not a stop sign. It indicates importance, not impossibility. The resistance you feel becomes a reliable guide, pointing toward your next breakthrough.

But knowledge isn't enough. Understanding these principles intellectually won't change your life. You need to embody them, live them, and practice them—even when, especially when, you don't feel like it.

So, here's what I suggest you do tomorrow morning: When that alarm rings, don't negotiate with yourself. Don't wait for motivation, don't check your phone, and don't hit snooze. Just get up and start moving. Take that first step, however small it might be. Remember, you don't have to feel like doing something to do it. You don't have to be motivated to take action. All you need is the decision—a commitment to show up, regardless of how you feel.

When I need to work on a task, I say to myself, *right now*. Notice I said "when I need" to work on a task, not "when I want" to work on a task; this is for starting something, making a call, or arranging a meeting. You see, you may think of doing it, but when? Don't give your brain time to negotiate; just do it right now.

Done is better than perfect. Action beats intention. Start now, adjust later.

Most motivational advice tends to fall short, often urging you to get excited, to pump yourself up, and to find your passion. However, passion without discipline is like a treadmill without a mat. It looks great in your room, but it won't help you get fit. There will be days when you don't feel passionate, moments when your motivation vanishes, and times when your enthusiasm fades. These are the moments that define your destiny; they are where champions are made.

It's fascinating how we rationalise our circumstances and create excuses. We excel at justifying inaction, and, for many, procrastination has become an art form. The more intelligent you are, the better you are at convincing yourself that now isn't the right time to act on something for your business or in life. But here's the truth: Time doesn't care about your excuses. It doesn't wait for your mood to improve or pause while you gather your courage. Time moves forward relentlessly, taking your dreams with it—unless you choose to move with it.

When you force yourself to work, even when you don't feel like it, you're doing more than just completing a task or checking something off your to-do list. You're making a deposit in your future. You're investing in your potential and building compound interest on your actions. Each time you choose discipline over comfort, you're not just winning today's battle; you're winning tomorrow's war. You're creating momentum that carries forward, building habits that compound over time, and developing strength that will serve you in countless future challenges.

Resistance

However, here's where it gets really interesting. The resistance you feel—the voice in your head telling you to wait, postpone, or delay—is actually a gift. Yes, you heard me right——that resistance is a sign of your personal growth potential. The stronger the resistance, the more important the task usually is for your growth. Have you noticed that you never feel resistant to things like watching TV, scrolling through social media, or engaging in mindless entertainment? That's because these activities don't challenge you; they don't push you to grow or demand anything from you.

The resistance you feel toward meaningful work is similar to the resistance that weights provide in the gym. Without that resistance, there's no growth. Without that tension, there's no transformation. The very thing that makes it hard is also what makes it valuable in helping you. This realisation changes everything. When you start to see resistance as a compass rather than a barrier, procrastination loses its grip on you. The presence of that uncomfortable feeling becomes a signal that you're on the right track—pushing against the boundaries of your comfort zone and, ultimately, growing.

Let's get practical: How do you force yourself to work when every fibre of your being is resisting? Many people make the mistake of tackling their biggest challenges head-on when their motivation is at its lowest. It's like attempting to lift your heaviest weight when your muscles are cold, a recipe for failure.

Instead, start small—ridiculously small. Make your goals so tiny that your brain can't argue against making them. Can't face writing that report? Commit to writing just one sentence. Can't motivate yourself to exercise? Promise to do stretching. Can't start that difficult project? Pledge to work on it for just 5 minutes. This approach isn't about how much work you accomplish with those tiny commitments; it's about breaking through the initial resistance. It's about creating a pathway to progress.

Once you start, something magical happens——the resistance begins to melt away. The task that seemed impossible becomes manageable, and the mountain that looked insurmountable turns into a series of small hills. This is where discipline transforms into self-respect. When you force yourself to work even when you don't feel like it, you send a powerful message to yourself. You affirm that your dreams are more important than momentary feelings. You declare that your goals matter more than your comforts. You prove to yourself that you can be trusted with your own aspirations.

Consider the implications of this in your business and life. Every time you break a promise to yourself, you weaken your self-trust. Every time you give in to resistance, you reinforce the habit of surrender. But every time you push through and show up, despite not feeling like it, you strengthen your character. You build what I call your reliability muscle, one of the most valuable assets you can develop because success in any field ultimately hinges on reliability.

Can you be relied upon to deliver, regardless of how you feel? Can you be trusted to show up, even when motivation is low? Can you be depended upon to follow through despite obstacles? The world is full of talented but unreliable people—those who could achieve greatness if only they worked consistently, those with amazing ideas who never follow through, and those who start strong but fizzle out when the initial excitement wears off.

That's the truth that transforms lives: Consistency trumps talent; reliability beats natural ability. Showing up every day outperforms sporadic brilliance. The person who works with discipline, even when they don't feel like it, will always outperform the person who only works when inspired. The most dangerous lies are the ones we tell ourselves, and one of the craziest is this: "I need to feel ready."

Nobody ever feels completely ready or perfectly prepared. The people you admire, the ones who've achieved remarkable things—they weren't ready either. They just started anyway.

We've been conditioned to believe that confidence comes before action, that we need to feel certain before we begin, and that we must eliminate all doubt before we take the first step (as we learned earlier in the book). But this is backward thinking. Confidence isn't the prerequisite for action; it's the result of action. Certainty doesn't come before the journey, but comes from the journey.

Imagine learning to ride a bicycle. No amount of study or theoretical understanding can replace the feeling of truly riding. Sure, you can delve into physics, watch countless instructional videos, or pore over manuals, but the real essence of confidence comes from the moment you hop on that bike and start pedalling. You gain confidence by taking action, stumbling, picking yourself back up, and pushing through even when you have a few scrapes and bruises. This cycle of learning applies to every aspect of life, especially in business!

You don't need to wait for the perfect moment to feel ready—just dive in! Think about public speaking. You don't become confident by waiting for the butterflies in your stomach to settle. Instead, you gain assurance by practising, even when your voice quivers; the same goes for the business realm. Don't wait for the stars to align: take bold steps, embrace mistakes, learn along the way, and adapt–all while pressing on through setbacks.

Here's a thought that might surprise you: The most accomplished individuals don't rely solely on motivation. They've separated their actions from their emotions, creating systems and habits that function on autopilot, no matter how they're feeling. They recognise that motivation is akin to changing weather; it often fluctuates. But systems, habits, and discipline? They are the steady climate that provides stability, reliability, and predictability.

When you stop asking yourself, "Do I feel like doing this?" and start asking, "Does this support my vision and what I'm committed to doing?" a remarkable shift occurs. The first question invites negotiation with yourself, while the second one prompts tangible action. The first question can easily empower your emotions, while the second one acknowledges them without letting them dictate your choices.

Every time you hit the snooze button, postpone an important task, or succumb to distractions, you're not just sidestepping discomfort: you're casting votes for the person you wish to become. Your future self will be moulded by the choices you make today. And here's where it gets truly fascinating—your brain is remarkably skilled at rationalising any decision you make. If you consistently favour comfort over growth, your brain will adapt to that choice.

Let's embrace growth! Choose action and witness the transformation within yourself. You're capable of so much more than you realise!

Fears and Small Steps

Fear in a new business and an established business is different for both.

One of the main fears for a brand-new business is not getting customers. "What if no one buys?"

Here is how it appears:

- Hesitating to launch because the logo, website, or product or service "isn't ready yet."

- Overthinking pricing

- Avoiding sales calls or outreach because of the fear of

being rejected

- Delaying marketing because of fear of being judged

- Feeling sick before posting your first social media ad or opening the doors

New owners often invest savings, time, and reputation into their business. When customers don't show immediately, it can feel like personal failure because of what they have put in personally.

Every business starts with zero customers. Confidence comes *after* action, not before. The more a task or activity is undertaken, the more confidence builds.

One of the main fears in an established business is the fear of losing what has been built.

Once a business is established, the biggest fear is no longer "starting"—it's losing everything you worked for.

"What if competition, the economy, or mistakes destroy what I built?"

Here is how it appears:

- Overworking to "maintain control"

- Fear of delegating because you've been burned

- Avoiding innovation because "it might break what's working."

- Anxiety when sales slow down, even slightly

- Stress around hiring or expanding

Now that the business supports employees, customers, family income, and reputation, there is *more to lose*, and the fear shifts from failure to stability.

But what if instead of feeling fear, you aimed for progress? What if instead of waiting to feel completely ready, you decided to be "ready enough"? The most successful people in any field aren't necessarily the most talented or the most intelligent. They are the ones who were willing to start before they felt ready. Look fear in the face and say, "I am going to do it anyway." They understood that being willing to be bad at something temporarily could lead to becoming good at it permanently. They recognised that imperfect action beats perfect inaction every single time.

Think about this: Every master was once a disaster, every expert was once a beginner, and every success story started with someone who didn't feel ready but began anyway. The difference between where you are and where you want to be is primarily determined by your willingness to act, even when you don't feel like it.

This brings me to another crucial aspect of forcing yourself to work: the compound effect of small actions. Most people overestimate what they can achieve in a day and underestimate what they can achieve in a year. They look for dramatic transformations instead of consistent progress and want quantum leaps instead of steady steps. However, life-changing transformations rarely happen in a single moment; they occur through the accumulation of seemingly insignificant choices.

Every time you push yourself to work when you don't feel like it, you're not just completing a task; you're building momentum. You're creating a force that makes the next right choice easier and the one after that even easier. Think of it like a spacecraft breaking free from Earth's gravity: the hardest part is the initial launch, which requires a tremendous amount of energy to overcome gravitational pull. However, once in orbit, maintaining that momentum becomes much easier.

The same principle applies to personal discipline. The hardest part is breaking free from the gravitational pull of your comfort zone. But once you build momentum, maintaining discipline becomes increasingly natural, and you don't want to stay in your comfort zone.

Here's what separates the exceptional from the average: Exceptional individuals have learned to fall in love with the process. They embrace the daily grind and find beauty in the mundane moments of discipline that many others avoid. Forcing yourself to work when you don't feel like it isn't just about willpower; it's about recognising that your feelings are often poor indicators, unreliable, of what's important.

Your feelings may tell you to stay in bed when opportunity is knocking. They may urge you to quit when a breakthrough is just around the corner or to give up when victory is within reach. This is why successful people let their goals, not their feelings, drive their actions. They understand that feelings are like clouds in the sky—constantly changing, sometimes dark and heavy; other times light and peaceful. But their commitment, discipline, and dedication are like the sun above—constant and unwavering.

Think back to the last time you pushed through resistance and did what needed to be done. Remember that sense of accomplishment, that quiet pride, that inner strength you experienced? These are the true rewards of discipline. Task completion is just a bonus; the real victory is proving to yourself that you can be trusted with your own dreams and can accomplish them.

But where most people get stuck is they wait for big moments, dramatic opportunities, or perfect circumstances to validate their worth. They don't realise that greatness is built in the small moments of choice that often go unnoticed. It's constructed in those early morning decisions before the world wakes up, in the late-night commitments when everyone else has gone home, and in those instances when every fibre of your being is screaming for comfort, but you choose growth instead.

Your potential for growth is directly proportional to your ability to handle discomfort. The more comfortable you become with being uncomfortable, the more you'll grow. The more willing you are to do what others won't, the more you'll achieve what others can't. This is why forcing yourself to work when you don't feel like it is such a powerful catalyst for personal growth. Each time you choose discipline over comfort, you're pushing the boundaries of what you believe is possible and redefining your limits.

What many people don't understand about achieving the extraordinary is that it's not about doing extraordinary things; it's about doing ordinary things exceptionally well. It's about doing the right thing, even when that's not easy, and showing up, even when you don't feel like it.

Think about it: Every significant achievement in human history was built on thousands of moments when individuals chose discipline over comfort. Every great invention, every remarkable discovery, and every amazing performance has a foundation of perseverance. To give you an idea, here are 2 examples of small business success stories:

Dynamic Automotive

Dynamic Automotive from Maryland, U.S.A., started as a single repair shop and over more than 30 years, grew into seven thriving locations. The founders discuss how they survive recessions, industry change, and staffing challenges by focusing on customer trust, community roots, and constant reinvestment in the business.

They didn't explode overnight; they compounded small wins over decades, staying committed through slow growth and tough years.

Reds Hair – Salon Owners Who Took Over During COVID

Reds Hair, located in Pukerua Bay, New Zealand, was taken over by two women, Jenna and Nic, **during the COVID-19 pandemic**—and at the same time, they both discovered they were pregnant. They had to juggle lockdowns, cash-flow pressure, and motherhood while learning to run the salon. Despite that, they turned it into a **successful, inspiring small business** featured as a success story in the industry.

They didn't wait for "perfect timing"—they built through chaos and life changes (https://www.kitomba.com/blog/success-story-reds-hair/).

The world belongs to those who show up consistently—not just when they feel like it or when it's convenient, but persistently and relentlessly. Most successful people understand that it's not about intensity; it's about consistency.

Remember, your future self is watching. Every decision you make today is shaping the person you'll become tomorrow. Each time you choose comfort over growth, you're endorsing under-performance. Conversely, every time you choose discipline over comfort, you're voting for excellence.

When you force yourself to work, even when you don't feel like it, you're also setting an example for others. You are showing what's possible and demonstrating that it's not the circumstances that determine outcomes, but the decisions we make each day.

The gap between who you are and who you want to be is bridged by your daily decisions—not by intentions, goals, or dreams, but by those moments when you choose discipline over comfort. Every time you make this choice, you're not just changing your actions but also your identity.

You're not merely becoming a different person; you're creating character that you can appreciate. This is the hidden power of forcing yourself to work when you don't feel like it. It's not just about productivity or achievement; it's about transformation, becoming the kind of person who can be trusted with great responsibilities, who can handle success when it comes.

At this point in the chapter, we've come to a moment of truth: Everything discussed—every principle, every insight—means nothing without action. Knowledge without action is like having wings but never choosing to fly. The question isn't whether you understand these principles, but what you will do with them. How will you plot your course? How will you transform these concepts into reality?

We are living in extraordinary times—times of opportunity but also unprecedented distraction. It has never been easier to access opportunities, yet it has also never been harder to maintain focus. The ability to push yourself to work when you don't want to is more valuable now than ever. Your discipline is the ultimate competitive advantage. The ability to focus and forge ahead is becoming a superpower among business owners.

Being a business owner is not reserved for the lucky or the gifted—it belongs to the bold. It belongs to those who act in spite of fear, choose progress over procrastination, and move forward even when the path is unclear.

If you're feeling stuck, you're not alone. But you do have a choice. Not to wait. Not to hope. But to move. Because the life and business you want are not waiting on the world—they're waiting on you.

The choice is yours. The time is now. The power is within you—use it. Act on it. Your destiny awaits on the other side of discipline. Your greatness lies beyond your comfort zone, and your legacy begins with your next decision. Choose wisely. Choose growth over comfort. Choose discipline over ease. Choose action over excuses.

In the end, we become what we repeatedly do. Excellence, then, is not an act but a habit, and that habit starts with your next choice.

Chapter 8
Take Control

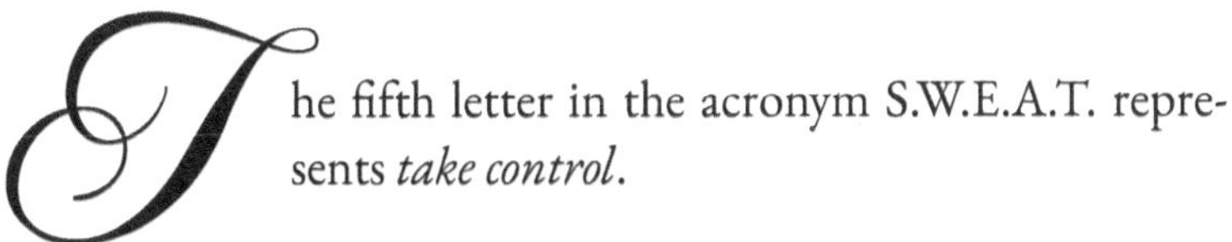

The fifth letter in the acronym S.W.E.A.T. represents *take control*.

"Success is not how high you have climbed, but how you make a positive difference to the world."
– Roy T. Bennett

Take control of your life as a business owner by embracing the power of ownership. Taking control starts with owning not just your business, but also your mindset, decisions, and results. There is no boss to blame, no corporate safety net to catch you, and no fixed path to follow. The sooner you embrace the idea that every choice you make, or fail to make, shapes your future, the sooner you can steer your life towards your vision.

Ownership means refusing to see yourself as a victim of circumstance and instead becoming the architect of your own opportunities. You need to take ownership of where you are and what stage you're currently in with your business's progress. So, if you feel stuck, you must acknowledge that you are in this position due to the decisions you made or didn't make, not someone else.

You can't blame external factors such as economic conditions, social influences, or family issues for your circumstances. Doing so will allow these external factors to control you or your business in the future. Embrace ownership to empower yourself and drive your business journey.

If you make mistakes, don't blame anyone. Use those mistakes as learning opportunities to help you move forward. Understand what happened but keep progressing and stop attributing blame to others for the actions you've taken or those you haven't. You need to take control of every stage of your business, and that control can start as early as the moment you wake up.

When you wake up, what you decide in those first moments will shape the look and feel of the rest of your day. Use this opportunity to focus on what you need to accomplish throughout the day. The key is not only when you wake up, but how you wake up. We all have the same amount of hours in the day, so be intentional with what you want to achieve that day. Create a morning routine, as stated before. Think about how to best use the day and don't overthink what needs to be done. Think with clarity and purpose but also feel excited that you have been blessed with another day with the freedom to make choices.

Don't wait to feel motivated; make this routine a daily habit. If you wait to feel driven, then when it doesn't happen, you stop and just roll out of bed. Starting your morning routine with intention relies on discipline, and this is a strength you need to practice consistently.

Jenny's Story

Deciding to leave her job, Jenny started her digital marketing agency out of passion. Initially, she accepted every client she could find, ranging from local bakeries to tech start-ups, believing that saying "yes" to everyone would lead to growth.

However, after two years, she found herself exhaustively busy. Her days were filled with back-to-back calls, she worked late into the night, and her profits began to shrink. Worse yet, she felt like a stranger in her own business, doing work that she didn't enjoy for clients who drained her energy.

One Friday, after losing a high-paying client's business, she sat down with her journal and asked herself: *"If I could rebuild my business from scratch, what would it look like?"*

Over that weekend, she got clear with herself: Jenny wanted to focus only on mission-driven start-ups, build a remote team, and work no more than 35 hours a week.

On Monday, she made the following transformative decisions:

- Let go of misaligned clients

- Doubled her rates for new projects

- Hired a virtual assistant to take over office tasks

- Created a 90-day growth plan focused on one niche

Six months later, her agency's revenue was higher than ever, her virtual assistant handled most of the day-to-day work, and she finally had evenings free.

Jenny learned that control wasn't about working harder—it was about choosing direction, setting boundaries, and designing a business that served her life.

You need to be comfortable with your choices and make decisions that align with your goals. Remember, you cannot blame anyone but yourself if you feel stuck. One of the strengths of being a business owner is the ability to acknowledge your mistakes and take responsibility for them. You just need to recognise the problem, rectify it, and move on. Don't dwell on your errors; instead, view them as part of your journey.

Everyone makes mistakes, even successful individuals. For instance, Thomas Edison failed thousands of times before achieving his goals. Look at your mistakes as essential steps in your journey, and that will help you move forward.

You must have clarity with your actions because, without clarity, control isn't possible. I have seen too many business owners operate in survival mode, constantly reacting to problems instead of pursuing a clear strategy to stop problems before they start.

Establishing Your Plan of Control

Developing a well-thought-out plan to lead your business is essential. You need a clear roadmap of where you want to go, including the strategy and the steps you need to take. This involves making the necessary calls and implementing effective marketing efforts; all of these are integral parts of your strategy and how you can take control of your business.

It's important to note that you don't have to do everything on your own—you can outsource certain tasks. However, outsourcing comes with its own set of risks, which is a part of being a business owner. Remember, everything carries some level of risk; life itself is full of uncertainties. Fortunately, there are tools and resources available to assist you.

Having a comprehensive plan to operate your business provides clarity about your goals and helps you visualise what control with your business and clients looks like for you. This control goes beyond financial aspects: it encompasses your lifestyle, relationships, health, and personal fulfilment. Once you have a clear picture and vision of your objectives, you should filter all opportunities through the question: "Does this move me closer to my vision?" We previously discussed the 80/20 rule, where 20% of your activities will yield 80% of your results. Therefore, it's crucial to assess whether any given opportunity aligns with your overall strategy.

Moving closer to your vision often involves facing unexpected opportunities that could be good or bad. While some of these opportunities may seem appealing, it's important to assess whether they will help you progress or divert you from your goals, remaining in control of the outcome. You need to determine if an opportunity is truly beneficial or if it might be a distraction as well. Reflect on the direction you are currently taking—does it satisfy your needs?

This opportunity could provide a chance to re-evaluate your business approach, innovate, and implement change. Ultimately, you are in control; you decide what path to take. Make a choice, or life will choose for you. Having a clear strategy is crucial. It's not about working more hours but finding alignment with your desired outcomes. Don't let new opportunities pull you off course if they don't align with your business plan.

One key strength of business ownership is the ability to say no to what doesn't matter, which allows you to say yes to what truly does. What doesn't matter are distractions that take you away from your focus and the energy necessary to create growth. When you say **yes** to what doesn't matter, you are automatically saying **no** to something that *does*—whether you realise it or not. Some examples of what doesn't matter to small business owners are:

- Perfect branding: Spending too much time perfecting the logo, brand colours, and web design early on. Customers *care more* about what you can provide than your logo design. Instead of spending 3 weeks perfecting a logo, time should be spent making offers to clients or customers.

- Doing everything yourself: Business owners often try to be the bookkeeper, marketer, salesperson, and manager. This may have been ok in the past: however, with improved technology, online collaboration, and the availability of professionals, owners should delegate anything that takes away their time from working on their business.

- Fancy office equipment or tools: If what you have in your business is sufficient, don't get caught up in the latest printer designs. This will impact your cash flow by diverting funds that should be spent on growing the business.

- Being busy instead of productive: If the website is being tweaked for the 10th time, it gives the false impression of being productive. This is a trap as it hides what is necessary to grow the business, such as sending follow-up emails, making calls, or refining your social media message to what resonates with potential customers.

- Trying to serve everyone: As mentioned earlier, trying to serve everyone can result in failing to adequately serve anyone. This approach can quickly lead to burnout and stress, leaving little energy for growth or business maintenance. The key to success lies in providing more value to your current niche market and learning to say no to those who fall outside of it.

These are all traps distracting business owners from doing important things, the tasks that matter. These traps aren't bad: they just don't drive revenue, growth, or customer loyalty.

End Every Day With a 5-Minute Clarity Check

Ask:

- What moved the business forward?

- What wasted time?

- What will I eliminate tomorrow?

- What will I double down on?

This builds self-awareness and discipline.

Build Time Blocks, Not To-do Lists

To-do lists sound great; however, more is generally added than what can be finished. Use time blocks instead by allocating:

- 1 hour → sales

- 1 hour → fulfilment

- 30 minutes → marketing

- 30 minutes → admin

Time blocks force focus and stop perfectionism.

Follow the 80/20 Rule

Focus on the 20% of activities that create 80% of growth:

- Sales

- Customer service

- Marketing

- Improving product/service

- Building relationships

Everything else is support—not the main event.

I've experienced this distraction in my own business. I once accepted a project that seemed helpful but ultimately didn't align with my core business principles. I realised I should have said no, and in the end, I had to step back and decline to provide the service, even though it left me in an uncomfortable situation with my client. Although this decision may have disappointed my client, it was necessary to maintain focus on my business vision and values. I've also seen businesses fold because the owner said yes to anyone and everyone and couldn't deliver on their promises: this led to angry customers and a mental strain on the owner.

I soon realised from my own situation that I couldn't handle everything, and it would have been much easier for me to say no from the start than overextend myself. I wanted to be accommodating to everyone, which taught me a valuable lesson: I can't do it all. There are only so many hours in the day, and if something is draining my energy, I need to say no. As a business owner, it's crucial to learn to say no as much as yes regarding future business opportunities.

Building Systems

Building systems, rather than chaos, is essential for maintaining control in your business. This doesn't rely solely on willpower; it requires effective systems. Many people view willpower as simply positive thinking, but it's true, as described in chapter 7, that power lies in taking action. You need to establish processes because, without them, the operation depends too much on the owner's energy and attention. This creates a fragile structure that can collapse when the owner steps away for some reason.

So, what do I mean by systems? **A business system is a set of organized processes that help a business operate smoothly and consistently.** It's short, clear, and easy to explain to anyone. It's vital to create a folder of processes and procedures, either hard copy, digital, or both. Having worked with large organisations, procedures and processes must be in place, especially with changes such as new employees or retirements, so everyone understands both the expectations and the standards for the business to run. Processes and procedures ensure every customer or client receives the same level of service and product quality.

Consistency builds trust, strengthens your brand, and reduces the chance of mistakes caused by guesswork. An advantage of maintaining this is efficiency and time-saving. Procedures elim-inate "reinventing the wheel" each time you are working with a client. Employees (or even you as the owner) don't have to figure out how to do routine tasks every time. This saves time, reduces wasted effort, and increases productivity.

If you want your business to grow, you need systems that can handle more volume without breaking down. Processes make it easier to delegate, onboard new employees, and replicate success as you expand. Processes and procedures should be centralised documents that are available to anyone involved in your busi-ness. To help in this system development, here's a **simple 4-step framework** you can use to start creating processes and proce-dures in your business.

My tip is to start small. Don't try to document everything at once but aim to build one process per week. In a few months, you'll have a mini "operations manual" that makes your business run smoothly if you are away or unavailable.

1. Identify the Repetitive Tasks

Start by asking: "*What do I (or my team) do over and over again?*" Some examples are:

- Responding to customer inquiries

- Sending invoices

- Onboarding a new client

- Posting to social media

- Preparing orders/shipping

Pick 3–5 of the most common, time-consuming tasks first.

2. Document the Steps

Write down the exact steps you take—keep it simple and clear, like instructions a new hire could follow. Example (Customer inquiry response):

- Open email inbox

- Check for new inquiries

- Use a template for general questions

- If it's a sales lead, forward it to the owner

- Respond within 24 hours (very important)

Tip: Don't overcomplicate it. Bullet points are enough for these steps.

3. Where to Keep

Decide where you'll keep these procedures. Options include:

- A **Google Doc / Word doc** (simple, easy to share)

- A **binder/manual,** if you prefer paper

The goal is that anyone in your business knows where they can access them quickly.

4. Test, Improve, and Standardise

- Try following your own written procedure to see if it works.

- Give it to an employee to test clarity.

- Once it works, make it the *official way* to complete the task.

- Include a review date, either 12 months or 2 years, to review and change if needed.

Moreover, it's important for business owners to have an emergency plan in case something happens to them. If an owner might be out of action for months, how can they keep the business running? It's crucial not to leave customers disgruntled or promises unmet. A disaster recovery plan is as necessary as your everyday processes. Think about what would happen if you were out sick or had surgery for 3 to 6 months. Can the business survive without you?

Ensure that you have digital processes in place and consider outsourcing some services. Delegation is key, and sometimes it's important to let go of certain responsibilities to focus on others as the business owner. Establishing systems in marketing, sales, operations, and finance creates stability and frees up mental bandwidth. This stability will also allow you to focus more on working "on" your business instead of "in" it. Don't fall into the trap of having the business run you.

A proactive approach, as opposed to a reactive one, is essential. Being reactive is draining and tiring, so you need to have a vision and be aware of your surrounding environment. While you can't control what happens around you, you can control how you feel and how you respond.

For example, Rosa, a business owner, had poured every cent she had into her small café (pardon the pun). After heavy rain impacted the road outside her café, a road maintenance project blocked her storefront for months, and as a result, foot traffic vanished. At first, panic crept in—sales plummeted. But instead of letting the situation control her fate, she started redesigning her business model.

Within two weeks, she launched a "Coffee-to-Your-Door" delivery service, taking phone orders and hand-delivering cappuccinos to nearby offices. She didn't wait for the city to finish construction—Rosa made her own road to loyal and new customers. Resilience here wasn't about enduring the hardship; it was about taking control of the wheel when the road ahead disappeared.

Canva (Melanie Perkins Co-founder and CEO)

Proactively solving a problem before it exploded

Back in 2006, Mel Perkins taught design part-time at the University of Western Australia, teaching students how to use programs like Adobe Photoshop and Illustrator—professional tools designed for designers. While teaching, she noticed how frustratingly complex it was for her students to create simple visuals. She kept noticing the same thing:

- Students were *overwhelmed* by complicated menus.

- Simple tasks took hours.

- People quit because the tools felt intimidating.

She also noticed how "clunky" the systems were, whereby everything was done offline. If you were collaborating with a team or needed approval on a project, you'd save the file, email it to your boss, and wait for their feedback.

Her lightbulb moment occurred when she visualised interacting with teams in real time across the globe using a more user-friendly graphic tool. She became proactive in solving the problems rather than waiting for someone else to act.

The steps she took to become disruptive in a graphic environment dominated by Adobe, Google, and Microsoft were:

- Started small rather than trying to build an all-in-one design platform immediately. This gave Mel and her partner, Cliff Obrecht, an opportunity to establish Fusion Books, an online tool for schools to design their yearbooks and test the market.

- After hundreds of investor rejections, she had the confidence to pursue her dream.

- Travelled to Silicon Valley to meet a well-known investor ... Bill Tai, who, at one of his events, introduced her to Cameron Adams, a former Google designer and engineer. She recruited him as a technical cofounder —a move that gave Canva the engineering power it needed.

Today, Perkins and her partner Cliff are worth more than 8 billion dollars. None of this would have been possible without 4 key ingredients:

- A solid concept that addressed user needs.

- The vision to prioritise Fusion Books early on to validate their ideas.

- The patience to wait for the right tech talent to join and develop the product.

- The courage to pitch in Silicon Valley and pursue their dreams.

Today, Canva is:

- Valued around US$40 billion

- Used in 190+ countries worldwide

- A top employer in Australia

- A global leader in design software

- It all started with a simple Proactive Belief: Design should be accessible to everyone, over a Reactive Belief (competitors).

- Adobe and Microsoft introduced simplified, browser-based design tools *after* Canva dominated.

- They reacted to Canva's success rather than innovating beforehand.

- Video editing, presentation platforms all reacted late.

Melanie Perkins and Clifford Obrecht weren't programmers, didn't come from wealthy families, lacked connections, and weren't based in the U.S. They simply recognised a need in the graphic design market that had to be met.

The lesson here is to be proactive and solve a future problem before the crowd notices it.

Resilience in the face of uncertainty is crucial. It's about taking control of your life, not every outcome—especially in business, where many factors are at play. It means managing your responses to investor rejections, mistakes, and unexpected challenges.

The business owner who thrives is not the one who avoids challenges but the one who adapts with resilience. By concentrating on what you can control—your mindset, habits, and ability to learn—you can remain empowered regardless of circumstances. Your business plan serves as a map, providing you with a vision for your future. Mel had an 80-page business plan for her online graphic platform.

"A goal without a plan is just a wish." – Antoine de Saint-Exupéry

Mel embraced the S.W.E.A.T. principle during her business journey through:

- Strength

- Weakness

- Energy

- Action

- Take Control

Embracing Your Authentic Self

If things don't work out, don't get disheartened; it happens to everyone. Life is unpredictable for all of us, but what matters is how you respond to it. Don't just sit back and wait for a magical solution; actively seek it out. Running a business is challenging but also exciting because it's your idea, your innovation—it's your baby. Freedom in business ownership means taking control and responding in ways that align with your ambitions and goals.

If your response doesn't lead to the desired outcome, consider it a learning opportunity and pivot. Resilience is vital in these moments; without it, you may find yourself looking to others for solutions instead of relying on your competence to solve problems. While you can seek assistance, relying too much on others can undermine your confidence and ability to tackle challenges independently.

The best gift you can give yourself is to be you. Embrace your individuality. In a society that often pressures conformity, especially in business, staying true to yourself can be challenging. When we honour our authenticity, we not only enrich our lives but also inspire others to do the same.

Lizzo's Inspiration

Lizzo is an American singer, rapper, songwriter, and flutist known for her powerful voice, energetic performances, and messages of self-love and confidence.

Before fame, Lizzo struggled with:

- Low self-esteem

- Body image issues

- Feeling "too different"

- Being told she didn't fit the mould for the music industry

For years, she tried to change herself—her appearance, her music style, her personality—to match what the industry expected.

But nothing worked. Lizzo felt disconnected and depressed.

The Turning Point

One day, she decided to be herself and not meet the media or the public's expectations.

She began:

- Writing songs that expressed her true feelings

- Celebrating her body instead of hiding it

- Being loud, joyful, emotional, and unapologetic

- Showing her real personality, quirks, humour, and style

Instead of trying to fit in, she leaned into her uniqueness.

What Happened Next was Transformational

Once she embraced her authenticity:

- Her music exploded globally

- She won Grammy awards

- Millions connected with her confidence and honesty

- She became a symbol of self-love and empowerment

- She created a new standard of beauty and acceptance in the media

People didn't just love her music—they loved the *truthfulness* in her energy.

Lizzo's authenticity didn't just change her life; it gave others around the world permission to say:

- "I can be myself."

- "I don't need to hide."

- "My uniqueness is my strength."

By honouring her authenticity, she became a source of inspiration for millions who felt different, insecure, or were hiding their true selves.

> *"To* be yourself in a world that is constantly trying to make you something else is the greatest accomplishment." – Ralph Waldo Emerson

To help in maintaining control of your business, here are 6 exercises you can use to gain clarity, control, and growth:

<u>Vision-Mapping Exercise</u>

- Write down your ideal business and life 5 years from now.

- Break it into categories: income, team, lifestyle, impact, and personal time.

- Reverse-engineer the steps needed to get there.

Time Audit

- For one week, track everything you do in 15-minute increments.

- Mark each task as low-level, medium-level, or high-level. *

- Start delegating or automating the low-level tasks.

* Low-level = Repetitive, day-to-day activities that keep the business running but don't directly move strategy forward.

Medium-level = Planning, marketing, and inventory control

High-level =Exploring new markets or product lines

The "Stop, Start, Continue" Review

- STOP: Identify tasks, habits, or offers that drain energy or don't move the business forward.

- START: Choose one new high-leverage action that will drive results.

- CONTINUE: Keep the habits and strategies that are working.

Ninety-Day Sprint Planning

- Choose 3 main business goals for the next 90 days.

- Break each goal into weekly milestones.

- Review progress every Friday and adjust.

- Write your progress in a journal.

Customer Feedback Deep Dive

- Interview or survey your top customers.

- Ask what they love, what they wish was different, and why they chose you.

- Use this feedback to refine your offer and messaging.

The "Freedom Test"

- Ask yourself: *If I were unwell or called away for 30 days, would my business still run?*

- Identify where it would break—then create systems to fix it.

- Write a procedure manual to document business processes.

Remember: You can't control every outcome, but you can control your mindset, habits, and responses to challenges.

Design a business that supports your life, not one that consumes it. The power is in your hands. Take it.

Chapter 9
Positive Mindset

*S*uccess in life requires dedicating time and effort. The most successful business owners make the most of their 24 hours by using them wisely to achieve their goals. You can do the same: to be a successful business owner, you need business skills such as effective time management, intentional actions, and a positive mindset.

"Success is not the key to happiness. Happiness is the key to success. If you love what you are doing, you will be successful." – Herman Cain

So, what is a positive mindset, and how do you achieve this?

This is an area that fascinates me in many ways. You need to look inward and understand why you think and behave the way you do. We are programmed from a young age to behave a certain way to receive acceptance, whether within our families or amongst friends. In a way, we become an extension of our loved ones and want to make them happy. However, do we make ourselves happy in the process?

We are told to live in the present moment, but what does that mean? It means not to dwell on the past or predict the future. God's loudest voice is silence, or whatever your belief is. So, what is silence? Silence is not being distracted by your external environment through noise or audible sound.

To help, here are 10 ways to help support a positive mindset and make progress towards your goals:

- **Use Your Mornings:** Start your day earlier and dedicate that time to your goals before you leave for work. Even if you need the first 10 minutes to clear away brain fog, mornings are ideal because you're less likely to be interrupted, well-rested, and nothing has derailed your focus yet.

- **Use Your Evenings:** Extend your bedtime by 30 minutes. Dedicate this time to reading or listening to a podcast that meets your business goals. Then, listen to chill-out music to relax and fall asleep.

- **Use Your Lunch Hour:** Instead of joining colleagues for lunch, pack your own meal, eat at your desk or a nearby location, and use the lunch hour to write, learn, or take steps towards your goals. Be consistent and make it a daily practice. This is your time, so use it and enjoy.

- **Use Your Commute:** Transform your commute into a goal-achievement exercise. *Listen* to podcasts while on the train or bus.

- **Cut Out One Activity:** Evaluate how you spend your time. Identify an activity you can eliminate to create space for goal-related tasks. Consider reducing TV, online games, or Internet browsing. You'll know which one to cut.

- **Prioritise Tasks:** Identify the tasks that will move you closer to your goals and prioritise them based on urgency and importance.

- **Become a Time Warrior:** Steve Chandler's book *Time Warrior* illustrates how to prioritise and allocate time for what truly counts. The Time Warrior isn't just about managing time; it actually provides the reader with gentle and simple tools to overcome their psychological blocks and become an honourable person of integrity.

- **Block Out Dedicated Time:** Schedule specific blocks of time for your goals. Treat these appointments with the same importance as meetings or doctor visits.

- **Be Flexible:** If something isn't working, adjust your approach. Learn from setbacks and use them as opportunities for growth. Life is unpredictable, and flexibility is key to adapting to changes and challenges.

- **Take Care of Yourself:** Remember to prioritise self-care, including sufficient rest, exercise, and relaxation. A healthy mind and body are essential for sustained focus and productivity. Be in a positive frame of mind. You don't need more time; you need stronger reasons to act, so you use time more effectively. You've got this.

Facebook Groups for Ideas and Products

Know enough about the prospective customer and anticipate some of their needs, desires, wants, or pain points and how your business can help fulfil those. Find out as much as you can about them. One source is to join a Facebook group in your area or a group associated with your product.

Facebook groups can serve as a marketplace for businesses to promote products, services, or ideas to a targeted audience. It provides an opportunity for direct engagement and feedback from potential customers. They allow for discussions, sharing of experiences, asking questions, and seeking advice in a more focused environment than the broader Facebook feed. Even if you are new to the group, do a word search within the group to read previous discussions around the topic. Find out what people need or ask questions about what their concerns are. It's a great forum that you can access for valuable information.

Know your competition. Be clear about what your competition is and the advantages you have over them. Be aware of what they have to offer the community and make yours different in some way. If you are viewed as the same, you'll negotiate on price alone. Identify unique selling points (USPs) that set you apart and provide value to your target market: this could be through product features, pricing, customer service, or branding. Competing in a market effectively involves understanding your target audience, strategically positioning your offerings, and continually adapting to changes in the market environment.

Techniques and tools to apply for your success: 80% why, 20% how. Big enough to get out of bed and start your day. Could you make a difference in their life? Find out the most compelling reason to drive you to your best. As a persuader or salesperson, you must sell positive consequences if they buy and negative consequences if they don't.

People buy what they want, and they are motivated. This relates to a deep-seated desire where they can justify the purchase. People have to associate buying with pleasure and hope for an improved life. They will miss something if they don't buy your product or service. Sell the reasons they need to buy, not your reasons. Get them to change for their own reasons. Provide a quality product that meets their needs.

People don't buy products; they buy solutions to their problems. They associate your product with their answer. We control what people focus on by the questions we ask. Asking questions builds rapport. When you ask questions, it is your most powerful tool for influencing people. When you understand what people believe and how they make decisions, all you have to do is show that buying your product or service is consistent with those beliefs. That's all selling is!

What is the difference between success and failure in business? Compelling reasons. More of a demand and sense of urgency. Strong goals and beliefs to achieve them. Customers need to have a belief that buying your product or service will mean having their wants filled. Pain will go away and be replaced with the benefits of buying. Is it worth it ... opportunity cost? What will it cost if they don't buy? Recognise pain if they don't buy and pleasure if they do.

Use questions to control your focus. What are some empowering questions you could ask *yourself* and write in your journal? What are some questions that could put you in a positive mindset right before a *customer meeting*?

Empowering Questions for Yourself:

How can I encourage progress towards my goals today?

How can I turn challenges into opportunities?

What are my strengths, and how can I leverage them effectively?

What lessons can I learn from past experiences to improve myself?

Who can I connect with to support my growth and development?

What small actions can I take right now to make a positive difference?

What am I grateful for in my life, and how can I build on that gratitude?

How can I cultivate a mindset of abundance and possibility?

What is my vision for the future, and what steps can I take to bring it to fruition?

How can I challenge myself to step out of my comfort zone and grow?

Questions for a Customer Meeting:

What specific needs does this potential client have, and how can I address them?

How can I customise my pitch to align with their values and objectives?

What success stories or positive reviews can I share to demonstrate the value of my product or service?

What objections might arise during the meeting, and how can I effectively overcome them?

How can I convey confidence and enthusiasm while maintaining authenticity?

What questions can I ask the potential customer to understand their needs and preferences better?

How can I showcase my expertise and credibility in the industry?

What sets my product/service apart from the competition, and how can I effectively showcase these unique features?

How can I demonstrate my dedication to delivering outstanding, exceptional customer service, particularly in the after-sales process?

What are my key goals for this sales interview, and how can I ensure I achieve them?

Your potential customers will first evaluate you as a person and then consider what you have to offer. Your attitude towards your product will be reflected in your interactions, and your enthusiasm will be transferred to your customers and anyone you meet.

Remember to prioritise your mental health by taking time each day to do something that nourishes your soul, brings you joy, or recharges you. When we take care of ourselves, we can better care for others, and it will show in our interactions. It's essential to maintain a positive mindset to achieve success.

Developing Effective Communication Skills

Developing rapport with a prospective customer is crucial for building trust and establishing a positive relationship. Here are some strategies to help you develop rapport:

<u>Show genuine interest</u> in what the customer is saying by actively listening to their needs, concerns, and preferences. Give them your full attention without interrupting and demonstrate understanding by paraphrasing and asking clarifying questions of what they have said. Asking questions not only demonstrates your curiosity but also helps gather valuable information that can guide your sales approach. Put yourself in the customer's shoes and try to understand their perspective, showing empathy by acknowledging their feelings and concerns to validate their experiences.

<u>Look for common interests or experiences</u> that you share with the customer and use them as a basis for connection. This could be anything from shared hobbies to mutual acquaintances or similar professional backgrounds.

<u>Maintain open and welcoming body language</u> to convey approachability and receptiveness. Make eye contact, smile genuinely, and use gestures that signal warmth and friendliness.

<u>Identify shared goals or objectives</u> between you and the customer, emphasising how your product or service can help them achieve those goals. Highlighting mutual benefits strengthens the bond between you both.

<u>Be genuine and sincere in your interactions</u>. Customers can usually sense if someone is being insincere, so focus on building real connections based on honesty and authenticity.

Provide value by offering helpful insights, information, or resources that are relevant to the customer's needs, even if it doesn't directly lead to a sale. This demonstrates your commitment to their success and creates trust.

After the initial interaction, <u>follow up</u> with the customer to maintain the connection. This could be a simple thank-you note or a check-in to see if they have any further questions or concerns.

If you use email as a form of communication, it may lack the personal touch needed to build rapport. Sending emails involves not only the content of your message but also the tone, empathy, and understanding conveyed. How do we include these elements in your email communication to deepen your connection with your recipient?

In the email, instead of simply asking surface-level questions, consider asking open-ended questions that encourage your recipients to share more about their experiences, challenges, and goals. For example, instead of asking, "Did you receive my quote?" you could ask, "What are your thoughts on the quote I emailed you yesterday/last week, and how can I support you further?" This not only shows that you value their input but also opens the door for a more meaningful conversation. An example of a conversation is:

Follow-up on Your Quote Request

Dear [Customer's Name],

I hope this email finds you well.

I am following up on the quote I sent you last [day of the week]. I understand you're likely considering various options, and I wanted to ensure you have all the information you need from me.

The quote for [product/service] is attached, outlining the details we discussed. Please review it at your convenience, and feel free to reach out if you have any questions or need further clarification on any aspect of the proposal.

I'm committed to providing you with the best possible solution tailored to your needs, and I'm here to assist you every step of the way. Whether you have questions about the features, pricing, or customisation options, I'm ready to provide the answers you need to make an informed decision.

Your satisfaction is my priority, and I want to ensure that my solution aligns perfectly with your requirements. If there are any adjustments you'd like to make to the quote or if you need additional information, please don't hesitate to let me know. Thank you for considering [Your Business Name] for your [product/service] needs. I appreciate the opportunity to work with you and am excited about the possibility of helping you achieve your goals.

Please know that there's no pressure from my end. I'm here to support you in finding the solution that's right for you, whether it's with me or another provider. I'm looking forward to hearing from you soon.

Best regards,

[Your Name]

[Your Position]

[Your Contact Information]

Your response provides the necessary information, opens the door for further discussion, and demonstrates your willingness to engage with them on a deeper level. By adding: "Please know ....," you are adding empathy that acknowledges the potential stress or uncertainty the client or customer may feel and offering support without being pushy.

Another strategy is applying the art of persuasion. How do you incorporate this in your email responses? Consider the following questions with your communication:

How did you demonstrate empathy and understanding towards their situation and concerns?

Did you effectively convey the benefits of your services based on your own business experiences and challenges?

How did you tailor your advice and recommendations to address their specific needs and goals?

Were there any storytelling techniques or examples from your own experiences that particularly resonated with the client?

How did you follow up with the client to ensure they felt supported and confident in moving forward with your guidance?

Think about the specific pain points and challenges they may face and address them directly in your content. Additionally, don't hesitate to share real-life examples and case studies to illustrate key concepts and demonstrate the practical application of your advice.

If you've read through the pages up to here, congratulations; however, I left this chapter to last for a reason. I want this to be remembered not only as a business owner, but also for your personal life.

Many don't make business decisions and take action because of the "F" word, Fear. Fear is normal and part of every business owner's journey. Most successful business owners have faced fears, whether it's the fear of failure, the fear of rejection, or the fear of the unknown.

The first step is acknowledging the fear instead of avoiding or ignoring it. I felt fear while writing this book; my hope is that it will be the first of many, but I kept ignoring the feeling. Yes, you can shift your mindset in an instant.

Fear doesn't mean we're not capable—it simply means we're venturing into something unknown and challenging. It's a signal of growth rather than something to be avoided. Fear often arises when stepping out of our comfort zone or trying something new. Remember, our comfort zone is a beautiful place, but we won't grow there. When fear emerges, it's often because we're pushing boundaries and growing. It's a signal that we want this path, but a voice in our heads says we're not capable, and negative thoughts enter. Look at it as a tool for motivation and progress.

Gratitude

One way to shift your mindset to a more positive one and improve your well-being is to feel gratitude. Gratitude helps you focus on what you're thankful for. It involves recognising and appreciating the positive things in your life–big or small. It shifts your focus from what you *lack* in your business to what you *have*, naturally boosting your mood and helping you feel more optimistic.

Practical Ways to Feel Gratitude:

- **Gratitude Journaling:** Writing down 3 things you're grateful for each day helps your brain focus on the good things in life. It could be something big, like "a supportive friend," or something small, like "my morning coffee."

- **Gratitude Letters:** Writing a letter to someone who's made a positive impact on your life can be incredibly powerful; it will make you feel more connected and grateful.

- **Gratitude Reminders:** You can set reminders on your phone or put sticky notes around your room to prompt you to pause and reflect on what you're thankful for throughout the day.

- **Affirmation Cards:** Affirmation cards are individual cards with positive statements designed to help reshape negative self-talk, such as "I'm good enough and have the skills to run my own business."

Unlike journaling, affirmation cards are quick visual statements that you can quickly read before a difficult meeting with a client or customer, or if you need to start your day with encouragement.

Being a business owner means living with uncertainty. You can't control the economy, the market, or your competitors. But you *can* control your mindset. A positive mindset helps you recover faster, attract better opportunities, inspire your team, and make smarter decisions. It's not about ignoring reality—it's about approaching reality with a mindset that says, *"I can handle this, and I'll find a way forward."*

At the end of the day, your business will grow in the direction of your thoughts. So, think positively. Choose resilience. Choose to see challenges as opportunities. Because when you do, you'll not only build a stronger business—you'll build a stronger version of yourself.

In this book, we've walked through ideas, strategies, and perspectives that can help you grow, but the real transformation starts now—with you. Knowledge alone changes nothing; it's action that brings your dreams to life. Choose one lesson from this book and put it into practice today. Start small, be consistent, and watch how quickly progress adds up.

This isn't the end of your journey—it's a new beginning. Your growth, your confidence, your vision for the future, they're already unfolding. Keep going and never forget that you're capable of more than you've ever imagined. Don't wait for a magical break to inspire you to run and grow your business. The miracle you are waiting for to achieve this is you.

Acknowledgements

I'd like to thank the following people who contributed to this book: my editor, Blair Parke; my photographer, Sumico Photography; my book designer, Michael Rehder; and my husband—thank you for standing beside me through every stage of this journey. Your patience, encouragement, and belief in me gave me the strength to pursue my dream.

References

Adler, Mortimer J. 1997. *How to Speak, How to Listen*. New York: Simon and Schuster.

Allen, James. 2008. *As You Think*. Mumbai: Yogi Impressions Books Pty Ltd.

Bartlett, Steven. 2023. *The Diary of a CEO: The 33 Laws of Business and Life*. London: Ebury Edge.

Bristol, Claude M. 2019. *The Magic of Believing*. New York: Ixia Press.

Collins, Jim. 2001. *Good to Great: Why Some Companies Make the Leap... and Others Don't*. London: Century–Trade.

Collins, Jim. 2019. *Turning the Flywheel: A Monograph to Accompany Good to Great*. New York: HarperBusiness.

Friedman, Ron. 2021. *Decoding Greatness: How the Best in the World Reverse Engineer Success*. London: Simon and Schuster.

Funmadel Press. 2024. *The Canva Story: The Compendious Biography of an Australian Female Tech Entrepreneur, a Tech Pioneer, and the Founder of Canva*. Independently published.

Jeffers, Susan. 1987. *Feel the Fear and Do It Anyway*. London: Vermilion.

Klauser, Henriette Anne. 2001. *Write It Down, Make It Happen: Knowing What You Want and Getting It*. New York: Simon & Schuster.

Impossible Until It's Done| Nelson Mandela Speech. 2017. YouTube video. https://youtu.be/rV8UaGAVLSA

Robbins, Anthony. 2001. *Awaken The Giant Within*. London: Simon and Schuster.

Singh, Shubham Kumar. 2023. *You Become What You Think: Insights to Level Up Your Happiness, Personal Growth, Relationships, and Mental Health*. Independently published.

T, Steve. 2018. *Steve Irwin Biography: Wildlife Conservationist*. https://biographics.org/steve-irwin-biography-wildlife-conservationist/

www.ingramcontent.com/pod-product-compliance
Lightning Source LLC
Chambersburg PA
CBHW030931060726
47591CB00005B/1759